DREAMS OF GLORY:
Women of the Old West

Larry D. Underwood

Dageforde Publishing, Inc.

ISBN: 1886225-15-X
Cover Art by Angie Johnson Art Productions

Library of Congress Cataloging-in-Publication Data

Underwood. Larry.
    Dreams of glory : women of the Old West / by Larry D. Underwood.
      p.   cm.
    Includes index.
    ISBN 1-886225-15-X (alk. paper)
      1. Women pioneers—West (U.S.)—Biography—Anecdotes. 2. Frontier
    and pioneer life—West (U.S.)—Anecdotes. 3. West (U.S.)-
    -Biography—Anecdotes.   I. Title.
    F596.U55 1997
    978' .0099—dc21
    [B]   96-49505
                                                                          CIP

Dageforde Publishing, Inc.
941 'O' Street, Suite 728, Lincoln, Nebraska 68508-3625
(402) 475-1123 FAX (402) 475-1176
e-mail: dageforde.lnk@ispi.net
www.dageforde.com

Printed in the United States of America.
10 9 8 7 6 5 4 3 2 1

For my ladies,
Melissa Anne, Rebeccah Sue, & Beverly Sue

"Where is it now, the glory and the dream?"
William Wordsworth,
Ode. Intimations of Immortality

Table Of Contents

PART III: THE FEMALE'S BURDEN

Preface

The lawless frontier of the Old West drew not only restless men, but a number of restless women as well. Like the men, many were chasing dreams. The dreams of a better life, dreams of glory beckoned these women across the Mississippi, across the plains to their new lives, new beginnings, that all men and women searched for in the wild and woolly West of a century or more ago.

In this historic collection of women, readers will discover the dreams that drew women to the Old West. The hopes and the fears of such working women as Lottie Ables Pickett, Mollie Scott, Julia Bulette, and Octavia Reeves were precursors of great tragedy. Nevertheless, that great magnet, the dream of glory, enticed them into a life of reckless fervor.

A woman's pursuit of life in a man's world of the 1800s was never easy. For interfering in that "sacred" world, a woman often had to pay extreme consequences. Nebraska's Elizabeth Taylor and Wyoming's Ellen Watson; both led great lives, but suffered great tragedies.

Sudden loss of dreams and glory came in many fatal forms. The women in this study sometimes died by their own hand, sometimes by murder—or saw their men killed. In many cases, a woman's dreams of glory died with her husband. That is the way it was with Zerelda James, the wife of bank and train robbing desperado Jesse James. But Jesse

James also had a mother. And she, too, suffered the pain of loss when her son was killed.

Colorado's Allie Townsend was the wife of a lawman in Leadville, Colorado, when she was made a widow by a lawyer bent on practicing his own form of justice. And then there was Missouri's Glendolene Myrtle Kimmell, who fancied herself the soul mate of famous scout, stock detective, and hired gun Tom Horn.

Whatever their destiny, their fate, nineteenth century women of the West made the best of their lives. Their pleasures were few and far between. Life was hard, just as they suspected it would be. And, some gave up. But many more fought to survive, raise a family, and make a contribution to the Old West of more than a hundred years ago.

Acknowledgments

Appreciation is due to the historians—amateur and professional—who helped to pull together the information necessary to write this book. Especially essential were the librarians, both men and women, who searched newspaper files in Wyoming, Nebraska, and Montana.

If not for the news reporters of the last century, much of what went into this volume would have been nearly impossible to locate. For these "historians," we all owe a deep debt. In an age when newspapers are finding it more and more difficult to survive, we would all do well to remember that many communities have only one "historian," their local newspaper.

My family, as usual, gets a great deal of credit for my writings. My daughters and wife are a constant reminder of just how fortunate we all are to live in the twentieth century. Still, modern women continue to face trials and tribulations. And, as it happened in the 1800s, present-day women are survivors—making us sometimes wonder where the idea of "the weaker sex" arose.

My son, Brett, was in charge of scouring the libraries and historical societies in St. Louis, digging for elusive information. As always, he did a splendid job.

Finally, but certainly not least important, are the ladies at Dageforde Publishing. It is a joy to be associated with Linda Dageforde and her professional staff. Patience may be the keyword to having a book published. They have been very, very patient with me. I shall always be grateful for that patience, served with an equal helping of kindness.

Larry Underwood
HCR 82 Box 66A
Meppen, Illinois 62013

PART I

Women At Work

Painted Ladies

Lottie Ables Pickett
The Shooting of Sorrel Mike

Prostitution was a tough, unforgiving way to earn a living
in the old West. A young prostitute often began her trade
while very young and she grew old too quickly. By age 30,
the flower of youth had faded for most.

But not all made it to age 30. Venereal diseases, botched
abortions, too much bad whiskey, a killing laudanum habit,
and a pistol-packing customer full of whiskey and hate were
all ways in which a hard-working prostitute might not survive. Their final prospect was often a lonely grave in some
Western boomtown. And, in just a few years, the grave and
its forgotten occupant were both lost forever.

Guilt was a burden that weighed heavily on many of
these wayward women. Generally, they moved with the
frontier. When they first arrived, they were a welcome sight
for miners and boomers with pockets full of precious dust
and a heart full of loneliness. Then, as civilization overran
the frontiersmen, wives, and families moved West and began the campaign to do away with prostitutes and dance
hall girls.

Guilt was a weapon used to rid the Western towns of
these "evil types." Some of the women were able to make excuses for their occupation. Many of the young girls came
from poverty and found it next to impossible to rise above
prostitution. For others, the long-suffering guilt of prostitution was brought on for a host of reasons, none of which in-

volved poverty, but more likely came from the ills of any society, modern or historic.

Nevertheless, many of the bawdy women looked for a way out. One survivor was Nellie Talbott who became ill, probably with tuberculosis. And as her looks faded, she found work as a scrubwoman. At the other extreme was a prostitute known as Josefa, who stabbed a California client to death early one July fourth. She was tried for murder by a hastily assembled miner's court. Guilty! the men ruled. She protested that she couldn't be hanged. She was three months pregnant.

Was it so? Four doctors examined her. Three said she was. One said she wasn't. The miners ran the the lone doctor out of town and got on with the sentence.

About 4 p.m., later that very day, Josefa climbed unassisted onto a bridge, adjusted the noose, saw to it that her skirts were tied down for modesty's sake, sailed her flowered hat into the crowd and said goodbye to about 2,000 onlookers, including several customers. She smiled and stepped off into eternity. One sad observer commented later, "And girls were so scarce in those days too."

Some prostitutes looked to marriage to free them from the cribs, brothels, hotels, saloons, or sporting house where they plied their trade. If marriage didn't rescue them, saving enough money to buy and operate their own brothel or saloon was a possibility. Others might solicit for two or three younger prostitutes. Some had considerable success as abortionists. But for many, with all hope lost, suicide became their salvation.

Eleanore Dumont, called Madame Mustache because of a downy layer on her upper lip, fought her way to the top, operating a brothel for a while. In 1879, however, Dumont chose her way out of the oldest profession. From Bodie, the Sacramento *Union* announced, "A woman named Eleanore Dumont was found dead today about one mile out of town, having committed suicide."

Suicide may have been the way out for Butte, Montana, prostitute Mrs. Lottie "Sorrel Mike" Ables Pickett. Lottie helped make the news that cold, December 15, 1881. The *Butte Daily Miner* had the story: "An Unfortunate Woman on Park Street Fatally Shot."

Lottie's friends called her Sorrel Mike. She was named for a champion race horse that once visited Montana Territory. She had lived in Helena, plying her trade, before moving to Butte. In Butte, she lived in a small frame house about a block east of Main Street, just south of Park. Living with her was a girl named Dolly. She claimed to be Sorrel Mike's (Lottie's) younger sister.

Butte was a rough, tough mining town in December 1881. The railroad, the Utah & Northern, was completed to Silver Bow, a junction about seven miles west of present Butte. It provided an outlet to the main Union Pacific Railroad line to Ogden, Utah. There were stagecoaches coming and going at all times of the day. The miners knew how to extract money from the surrounding mountains. The "working girls" knew how to extract money from the miners.

One of those working girls was a redhead named Lottie Ables Pickett. But at age 30, that gnawing, bothersome feeling was more and more frequently slipping over Lottie like a dark cloud. Lottie felt so hopeless that she didn't care if she lived or died. But she wasn't willing to leave it up to providence. She wanted to encourage it some, prod it along.

So, about 3 a.m. on the cold morning of December 14, 1881, Lottie took her .36 caliber Smith & Wesson, placed the muzzle against her belly "about two and a-half inches to the right of and a little up from the naval" and pulled the trigger.

A Helena doctor, B.C. Brooke, was called in. He had treated Lottie before, only she hadn't been as successful in the past. He quickly examined her, probed for the bullet, and found it in perfect condition to the right of the spine and below the kidney. Lottie was still coherent when Dr. Brooke arrived, but her pulse began to fade.

What had happened? She said she quarreled with a man. She took out her pistol and he took it away and shot her. She didn't know him. He had a light moustache, wore a cap and a brown overcoat.

Dolly frowned, shook her head and said, "Lottie, you know that is not so; you did it yourself. Some innocent man may suffer for your talk; and you know you did it yourself."

Dr. Brooke knew of her past. In 1879 at Helena, just about the time she married a bartender named Pickett, Lottie overdosed on laudanum. When she stumbled into work under the heavy cloud of the drug overdose, her friends got her help and she lived. In the summer of 1880 she used morphine to try and end her life.

Now, a year and a half later, Dr. Brooke looked her in the eyes and told her to come clean on what happened. She probably would not live this time.

Dolly added, "You know you did it yourself."

Lottie, growing paler, neither affirmed nor denied Dolly's statement.

Dr. Brooke fumbled around in his bag and came out with morphia and hydrate of chloral. Lottie drifted off and the doctor left.

About daybreak, Dr. Brooke returned. Lottie's abdomen was swollen and painful from the internal hemorrhage. Dr. Brooke administered more morphia and other sedatives and Lottie remained unconscious most of the day.

After a while, Dolly told how Lottie had quarreled with a male friend. The friend had left Butte for Jefferson several hours before the shooting. Someone sent a buggy after him with orders "to go and return at full speed."

More of the story was revealed. Lottie had told the man she'd argued with that "she would show him" if he left. Dolly, the "sister," added that she thought the wound was accidentally inflicted.

Dolly explained that a man had left the house without paying for his wine. Lottie, according to this version, decided to stop the wine thief and pulled the Smith & Wesson from under her pillow. As she waved it around, he tried to take it away from her. The gun went off and Lottie was shot. Accidentally.

But no one seemed certain about what happened. In some ways the dying Lottie was speeding toward death and those around her were not interested in dragging anyone along with her. Dolly told the others how Lottie had tried to kill herself before, just days ago. Dolly took the bullets out of the Smith & Wesson "all except one, which she laid in the bureau." Everyone figured that was "the fatal messenger."

Lottie died about two o'clock Friday morning, December 16, 1881. The jury came together at 10 a.m. for the inquest. They determined that Lottie "came to her death by a pistol wound inflicted by some person unknown." The jury added: "It seems to be the general impression among several of the jurors, that the shot was not fired intentionally, if at all, by Miss Pickett herself. The position of the wound is such that the pistol must have been held in the left hand on the hypothesis of suicide which would seem to negate any such supposition."

Lottie's earlier attempts at suicide had clouded the issue. Even her friends said they figured she shot herself. But this time, they speculated that it was her intention to inflict "simply a slight flesh wound."

A confused reporter for the *Butte Daily Miner* fumbled around finally extracting a sort of conclusion about the death. He wrote:

"In view of all the circumstances the theory first advanced that there was a man in the case, and that the pistol was accidentally discharged in a struggle for its possession, seems the most plausible. However, this may be, the facts are still involved in such uncertainty that it is not at all impossible that a murder has been committed, as declared by the deceased in her last coherent statement."

A small item appeared on the front page of the *Butte Daily Miner*, December 17, 1881: "Lottie Ables, alias Lottie Pickett, will be buried today at 2 o'clock."

The sorry saga of Lottie Ables Pickett, alias Sorrel Mike, was only one of many discouraging tales of the prostitute's life in the West. Scorned in the light of day, praised under the shield of darkness, it was a rare woman who took up the profession and survived it unscarred. In an age when help was not always there for those stricken with depression and suicidal tendencies, the woman called Sorrel Mike found little solace from anyone. Her repeated attempts at suicide, cries for help—resulted from ignorance, uncaring people, and the stigma of being a prostitute in the wild and woolly West.

ഇൗരു

Bibliography

Brown, Dee. *The Gentle Tamers: Women of the Old West*. Lincoln, University of Nebraska Press, 1968.

Buck, Franklin. *A Yankee Trader in the Gold Rush: The Letters of Franklin A. Buck*. Kathleen A. White (ed.). Boston, Houghton Mifflin, 1930.

Burlingame, Merrill G. *The Montana Frontier*. Helena, State Publishing Company, 1942.

Butler, Anne M.. *Daughters of Joy, Sisters of Misery: Prostitutes in the American West 1865-90*. Urbana, University of Illinois Press, 1987.

Butte Daily Miner, August 28, 1879.

Butte Daily Miner, September 20, 1879.

Butte Daily Miner, July 31, 1880.

Butte Daily Miner, December 15, 1881.

Butte Daily Miner, December 17, 1881.

Dunlop, Richard. *Doctors of the American Frontier*. New York, Ballantine Books, 1962.

Montana, *A State Guide Book*. Federal Writer's Project. NY, The Viking Press, 1939.
Sacramento *Union*, September 19, 1879.

Inez Maybert

In the Dark Valley

Sad stories were common across the panorama of the beautiful, yet lonely, American West of the 1800s. Tragedies were etched in the minds of the folks who lived during the period. Frontier newspapers often recorded the tragic tales, sometimes stripping the players down to their bare thoughts and feelings. One such tragic testimony came from the *Butte Daily Miner* dated Friday, November 11, 1881. It involved the sordid suicide of Inez Maybert who worked at a "well-known house of Park Street."

Here, then, is the short history of Inez Maybert as recorded in the *Butte Daily Miner*, author unknown:

IN THE DARK VALLEY

Suicide by Morphine of Inez Maybert on Park Street

At five o'clock yesterday afternoon a young woman in this city died from an overdose of morphine. Behind the plain statement of facts lurks a romance, woven of man's cruelty and woman's shame, in which the despair of a heartbroken girl finally drives her to destroy a life which had ceased to be other than a continual agony. At a well-known house of Park street an inquest was held last night, and a verdict returned of death from an overdose of morphine. Dr. Thompson, the Coroner, sum- moned the following jurymen: J. C. Baker, B. McGinley, John O'Meara, E. McLaughlin, J. J. Cable and Walter Eddy. The language of such a verdict is mysteriously suggestive of many possibilities of good or evil, but as regards Inez Maybert, it is known with reasonable certainty that her rash act was caused by the scorn of a man she loved. As she lay yesterday afternoon in an almost dying condition she called continually on the name of a man about town who was at one time her friend, but who, it is said, had maltreated her of late. Word was sent to him, but he is said to have answered with an angry oath. After death an ounce bottle of morphine, nearely [sic] empty, and a note was addressed to Gussie, a friend with whom Inez had passed her last night, and was in substance as follows:

> To Gussie I want you to do as you always said you would bury me all in black. Tell (the man) he may thank himself for this.
>
> If there is any such thing as haunting I will haunt him to his deathbed.
>
> INEZ

The facts are that the deceased had been drinking heavily for some days, and attempted to kill herself, with morphine, but was prevented by several of her male friends, in which cabin she was at the time. The ensuing night she spent with her friend Gussie, whose testimony threw much light on the matter. About nine o'clock yesterday morning Inez arose, and instead of going to her own room, as she said she intended doing, sent a Chinaman uptown for laudanum. It is supposed that she took the laudanum about eleven o'clock. About two o'clock her friend Gussie found her lying on a sofa, in a helpless condition, and breathing very heavily. Gussie supposed her drunk, and did not become alarmed until about three o'clock when a physician was sent for. But it was too late. After having called for a man already alluded to, as long as she could speak, she became insensible and died about five p.m. What could be truer or more appropriate in such a case than the pathetic lines of Hood written on the death of a London Magdalen, breathing as they do desperate misery and wild longing for something different if no better. As of her, it may be said of Inez,

> "In she plunged boldly,
> No matter how coldly
> The dark river ran."

℘Ↄℭℛ

Bibliography

Butte Daily Miner, November 11, 1881.

Mary Forrest Scott
Murder in Butte

Butte, Montana Territory, boomed in 1864 when gold was discovered. Boomers came from all points of the compass. Butte quickly became one of the great mining centers of the world. Located on a high plateau (5,716 feet) of the Rocky Mountains, the mines at Butte at one time over the next several decades were to yield gold, silver, copper, manganese, lead, and zinc.

Soon, Butte grew to be a community where a miner's money would buy anything. Endless veins of copper discovered in the early 1870s added to the boom town wealth. Butte became one of the biggest, brawlingest mining towns of the era.

At various times there were gambling houses that stayed open twenty-four hours a day. Two thousand miners and gamblers could play in one of these giant gambling houses at the same time.

One bar needed fifteen bartenders just to keep the beer and whiskey flowing. One poker player boasted of winning a $25,000 pot. And there were other tales of gambling at this mining town where money flowed easily.

One section of town noted for its parlor houses offered girls for sale. Molly Demurska had the the finest place and the prettiest gals in Butte. Someone looking for female company might find it at a dance hall or dance saloon near the bars and gambling houses.

But the Butte that Mollie and Joe Scott found in July 1880 was not overly exciting to them. They'd been chasing boom towns for several months now. They were in the Black Hills trying to eke out a living. Mollie was pretty and pleasant enough. She was about twenty years old when she married Joseph Scott. But Joe Scott was a mean one, and he was jealous of his young wife. He had a reputation as "a dangerous character."

After the mining camps and gambling tables of the Black Hills, the Scotts decided to move on. They tried Helena for a while, but had some bad time there. An altercation occurred at the Cosmopolitan Hotel. The night clerk at the hotel insinuated that Joe and Mollie were not man and wife. Joe, noted for his bad disposition, figured he needed to react for his twenty-year-old wife, Mollie. The night clerk persisted and would not allow Joe and Mollie, who he figured was a lady of the night, to take a room together at the hotel. In the end, the law was called. The result was that Joe and Mollie were arrested and charged.

It took a few days, but Joe Scott proved that Mollie was his lawfully wedded wife. They were man and wife, not what the night clerk mistook them for. All charges were dropped and apologies were made.

Still perturbed at Helena, its hotel night clerks, its law, and its jailers, Joe and Mollie Scott left the Helena jail and headed for Butte, some sixty-five miles southwest of Helena. They had no intentions of staying in a town with people who had mistreated them.

Butte was a new town for them. They'd make a go of it. Get a fresh start. Prosper. The Scotts had no more than arrived in Butte when Mollie took employment at the Union Dance Saloon. She was assigned a private room just down the hallway off the main ball room. For a fee, she and the other dance hall girls would dance with lonely, loveless miners.

Generally, the dance hall was a large room. A bar stood at one end and one observer noted that champagne sold for $12 in gold per bottle. Other drinks went for twenty-five to fifty cents each. Some patrons named their poison, preferring to call it "Tangleleg," or "Ligntning," or "Tarantula juice" rather than whiskey.

The bar where the girls sat waiting for a dance was enclosed so that customers could not get behind it. This area was usually crowded as customers pushed forward eager to dance with a certain girl. While a dancing girl did not expect to fall in love, there was nothing to keep a romantic, whiskey-laden fool from imagining an affair with one of the friendly, smiling dancers.

From behind the barrier then, the women, sometimes called "hurdy-gurdies," sat waiting. Usually, they were dressed in the best clothes they could afford.

Nearby, some of the dance halls had a raised orchestra and when the music struck up, someone called out, "Take your partners for the next dance." Men with tickets they'd purchased now came forward to select their dance mate. They were careful to be polite, as was the custom of the day, and invited one of the ladies to dance. When this was done, all took their places and waited for the dance to commence.

Thomas Dimsdale observed these ladies in Montana and described a first class dancer: "She is middle height, of rather full and rounded form; her complexion as pure as alabaster, a pair of dangerous looking hazel eyes, a slightly Roman nose and a small and prettily formed mouth. Her auburn hair is neatly banded and gathered in a tasteful, ornamented net, with a roll and gold tassels at the side."

Why it was enough to make a love-hungry frontiersman spend not just a dollar, but all his dollars just to see her smile as she danced around so daintily. And who could blame him?

Dimsdale recalled, "How sedate she looks during the first figure, never smiling till the termination of 'promenade, eight,' when she shows her little white hands in fixing her handsome brooch in its place, and settling her glistening earrings. See how nicely her scarlet dress, with its broad black band round the skirt, and its black edging, sets off her dainty figure."

The dancers were not necessarily beauties. It was the exception, more than the rule, to find a "pretty" dancer. Dancing was hard work. "Twenty-six dollars is a great deal of money to earn in such a fashion; but fifty sets of quadrilles and four waltzes, two of them for the love of the thing, is very hard work," noted observer Dimsdale.

And then someone calls out "gents to the right," and "promenade to the bar." The dance is over.

Most men in the community frequented the dance halls. Dimsdale claimed, "You can see Judges, the Legislative corps, and every one but the Minister. He never ventures further than to engage in conversation with a friend at the door, and while intently watching the performance, lectures on the evil of such places with considerable force; but his attention is evidently more fixed upon the dancers than on his lecture."

And Dimsdale also noted, "As might be anticipated, it is impossible to prevent quarrels in these places, at all times, and, in the mountains, whatever weapon is handiest—foot, fist, knife, revolver, or derringer—is instantly used." (Dimsdale, Thos. J. *The Vigilantes of Montana, or Popular Justice in the Rocky Mountains.* Virginia City, MT, 1866. pp., 8-13.)

Mollie worked through the weekend at just such a dance hall. Joe was free to gamble, drink, or visit Mollie's or other dance halls in town. But on Tuesday evening, Joe became upset with Mollie. She had gone to work at the allotted time. The heat of the day had been cooled as a gentle breeze pushed down from the nearby mountains. Mollie was dancing and enjoying her work. And the night slipped away.

Soon it was midnight and then, about a half hour later, Joe and Mollie had a disagreement.

The lights flickered in the ball room. A violin screeched a song and most of the dancers were subdued by now—too much dancing; too much booze. No one paid much attention to Joe and Mollie in the smoke-hazed room. But their conversation became animated. Those sitting close by heard Mollie say she wanted to go to another dance hall just "a few doors distant." (*Butte Daily Miner*, Aug. 5, 1880.)

Joe protested. She couldn't go. His hand flashed out and his fingers locked around Mollie's wrist. Mollie yelled at him, not because of the iron grip on her wrist, but because he was now dragging her toward a door at the back of the Union Dance Hall.

The door opened into a hallway. Still Joe held onto Mollie, half dragging her now toward her room. Joe's blood was up. How dare this woman not obey him. Inside her private room, Joe violently turned her loose. He shut the door.

Mollie probably knew she was in bad trouble. She may have even trembled as Joe stood over her, his rage boiling over.

In the dance hall, there were men and women dancing and smiling. Somehow over the hours, the women had gotten more beautiful. The sour whiskey breaths of the men smelled sweeter now, or was hardly noticeable at all. Certainly, the musicians played more melodically. No one paid much attention to the occasional screech of the violin. Some on the floor were thinking they could fall in love with their dance partner.

No one heard any sounds from the room that Mollie and Joe had disappeared into. There was no lull in the dancing. The music went on uninterrupted. About five minutes ticked by.

A reporter for the *Butte Daily Miner* (Aug. 5, 1880) recorded what happened next. "The loud, sharp report of a revolver rang through the building and hushed into silence the revellers in the dance hall."

The dancers sobered some and began mumbling to each other about what had occurred. No doubt; it was a pistol shot. And it came from the back of the building.

In an instant, Officer Micklejohn was through the front door and into the main ballroom. He'd heard the shot from outside. Several at the back of the room near the door to the hallway motioned the lawman toward the sound of the gun blast.

Micklejohn stepped into the hallway and, just as he did, Joe Scott stepped from Mollie's room into the hallway. Joe's face was twisted and flushed.

Micklejohn pulled his revolver and cocked the hammer. Punctuating this action, he called out, "What have you done?"

Joe said nothing, but began sliding along the hallway wall, edging ever closer to a back door.

"Stop!" Micklejohn ordered. But Joe Scott continued backing toward the rear entrance.

Micklejohn wasn't sure what had transpired. Had Scott killed someone? Had he missed? Micklejohn continued toward the door that Joe had stepped through. He couldn't stop Joe Scott with a bullet until he saw what was in the room.

At the door, Micklejohn pushed it open. There in the middle of the floor on her back lay Mollie Scott. There was blood on the floor and some on the wall. Mollie's beautiful 20-year-old face was half gone, blown away by a big bullet from Joe Scott's pistol.

Officer Micklejohn had seen enough. He spun and pushed by those in the hall, headed for the back door through which the killer, Joe Scott, had fled. He was just steps behind as Joe left the building and began running southwest from the Union Dance Hall.

The night was black as the two men scampered down an alley and across the lower end of Main Street. Micklejohn lost sight of Scott. He was not to be found. The *Butte Daily Miner* reported that Joe Scott was "lost sight of in the rolling round of the hydraulic claims in that neighborhood." (Miner, Aug. 5, 1880.)

Back at the Union Dance Hall, men and women gathered around the door to Mollie's room. They hardly knew her. Mollie had been among them for less than a week. Still, they had a lot in common with young Mollie. And the sorrow they felt now for Mollie was as much for themselves as it was for her.

A large dragoon bullet had killed her. The ball entered the right cheek below the cheekbone and took out six teeth. The lead projectile continued its damage, moving along a path that took it upward to where the skull and the head join. Finally, the bullet stopped just under the skin at the back of the neck.

Some speculated that the spinal cord must have been damaged. Mollie never spoke nor moved after being shot. Her breathing lasted for only a short time as the blood continued to pump from her body and life slowly left her.

The *Butte Daily Miner* (Aug. 8, 1880.) correspondent wrote, "The murderous bullet did its work only too well and the poor fallen woman made the last sacrifice it was in her power to make, the sacrifice of her life lost through her love for the man who she had cheerfully supported from the gains of her arduous calling, and for whom she would cheerfully have risked her life."

When the dawn came to Butte again, it was Wednesday, August 3. Some of the girls had gotten a nap; others had not slept. They were busy preparing a special sendoff for young Mollie Scott. Finally, about 9 a.m., Mollie was ready.

She had been cleaned up. The dried blood had been wiped from her face, head and neck. Her fine hair was washed and dried, then combed. Mollie was laid out in a beautiful white dress. On her delicate hands were kid gloves. Her hands were crossed over her breast. The bitter young reporter from the *Butte Daily Miner* viewed the body and then withdrew to write his feelings about Mollie and her friends' predicament.

Describing the scene at Mollie's early morning wake, he wrote, "Gathered around were several women of her class, all suffering the trepidation which invariably overcomes them upon the occurrence of such tragedies for it is only then that they appear to realize their true position and understand the constant danger for which they are exposed in the brutal and uncontrollable passions of the men whom they make at once their masters and companions."

It is likely that about the only ones to attend her 2 o'clock funeral later on August 3 were "several women of her class," all grieving for Mollie and themselves.

Joe Scott eluded Officer Micklejohn in the hours following the 12:30 a.m. murder of Mollie Scott. Later that day, however, it was a different story. Scott slipped on board a freight wagon bound for the railroad construction terminus some miles out of Butte. [Butte was scheduled to be the railroad terminus during 1881.] Men looking for him rode out to a point below Silver Bow and checked the wagon. Captain E.C. Owen and Mr. Dick Dickinson captured Scott. He did not put up a fight.

Scott was armed with the big dragoon revolver. One shot had been fired from it.

Back in Butte, Scott was taken before Justice Barret. The inquest held earlier in the day ruled that Mollie "came to her death from a pistol fired by Joseph Scott in a willful and felonies manner." At the hearing, Scott waived examination. "He was," according to the *Butte Daily Miner*, "immediately sent below to the county prison, as the state of feeling on the street was such that to attempt to keep him in custody in Butte over night would have been a dangerous experiment."

ഇൗരു

Bibliography

Dimsdale, Thos. J. *The Vigilantes of Montana, or Popular Justice in the Rocky Mountains.* Virginia City, MT, 1866.

Butte Daily Miner, Thursday, August 5, 1880.

Myths after Morphia:
A Small Dose of Opium and Morphia

Opium, known since at least 5000 B.C. as a painkiller, was a cure-all in the American West of the 1800s. It was prescribed and used by doctors for many ailments. If a gunfighter was wounded, the doctor administered some form of opium. If a bronc buster broke a leg, opium was the cure. Cancer, fever, tuberculosis, sore feet, toothache, and insanity could all be "cured" by opium.

An alcoholic or someone addicted to cigarettes could be cured by the opium method. And doctors used opium to cure opium addiction.

And social problems? Cure the alcoholic and crime would disappear. Laborers worked better when using opium and it calmed their nerves. The poor couldn't afford alcohol, but opium, morphine, and laudanum were cheap and within their financial means. In addition, the store owner, minister, or lawyer who used drugs would not have the telltale breath of an alcohol user.

"Female complaints" were treated with opium. One medical journal claimed that two to three times more women were addicted than men. To quiet a restless baby, or one that was teething, or had a little rash—you guessed it: "Mother Bailey's Quieting Syrup" laced with opium.

Patients were encouraged to treat themselves. In the 1890s, opium sold for forty cents for two ounces. Laudanum in a two-ounce bottle sold for eighteen cents. And Sears, Roebuck would sell the hypodermic syringe to administer the drugs for $1.50. No prescription was required.

McMUNN'S ELIXIR OF
O P I U M

Is the pure extract from the drug, from which all the hurtful properties are removed and the medical ones retained. No headache, costiveness or sickness of the stomach attend its use. Price 50 cents. All druggists.

It wasn't necessary to label the bottle with the ingredients. Would the ailing cowboy have taken a dose of Cram's Fluid Lightning if he'd known it contained not only oil of mustard and cloves, but *ether, opium, and alcohol*?

The morphine or opium could be drunk, chewed, or injected. Never was it appropriate to smoke opium. That was an Oriental thing looked down on in American society.

ഇ൦ർ

BIBLIOGRAPHY

Butte Daily Miner, November 11, 1881.

Died for Love

Women living in many frontier communities had similar problems. Suicide and shootings seemed far too regular a way for a 19th Century frontier woman to die.

Here then are the cases of two more Montana women, Annie Elliott and Polly Cunningham, as recorded in the November 5, 1881, *Butte Daily Miner*, author unknown:

A private letter from Lewis (Montana) to a party in Eureka incidentally mentions the death of two women at that place last week who were well known here. One was Annie Elliot (Big Mouthed Annie), and the other Polly Cunningham. The latter is alleged to have suicided with strychnine. Annie is said to have been accidentally shot and killed by interposing in a quarrel between her "fellow" and another man. Just as the opposite party was about to shoot, she is stated to have placed herself before her lover and received the shot intended for him through her heart. If these incidents are correctly reported, the atmosphere of Lewis is proving very unhealthy for the "girls," three having been "laid away" there within as many weeks. Eureka *Sentinel*

Calico Cats

The great number of prostitutes living in the towns and cities of the West were white. But women of color were not uncommon in the American West. Mexican women worked the bars and brothels of the Southwest. Chinese women could be found in the Rocky Mountain states and territories. In addition, Spanish Americans, Native Americans, Asiatics, and African Americans could be found in many frontier towns or coastal cities. They particularly abounded in towns built on mining. In the 1850s, San Francisco boasted women from all over the world. Lonely men with too much money were prime targets for the burgeoning flocks of women—foreign and native—who came on shore with the arrival of every ship—be it from New York, New Orleans, London, Le Havre, or Shanghai.

As for black women and others of color, they experienced many of the same prejudices. Black prostitution in the West increased with the end of the Civil War. And, just as in the eastern United States and some other countries of the world, African-American girls had to take lower paying, lower rung jobs. Prostitution was a likely place to start. Certainly, it had its risks, but it provided a roof over one's head and food to eat. And, of course, one need not be able to read and write or have special training for the occupation. An occasional beating by a drunken customer, the threat of venereal disease, and being forced off the job after age thirty, were things prostitutes tried to not think about. Most hoped to make enough money to someday retire and lead a more respectable life.

Julia C. Bulette

One mixed-blood woman, Julia C. Bulette, was one of the best known prostitutes on the frontier West. Some said the exotic beauty was Creole, coming from Liverpool, England, [Or was it London?] by way of New Orleans. Others have her born in the West Indies or perhaps Louisiana. When was she born? One source claims 1832.

Jule, as she was known to her friends, moved with her family from England, or the West Indies, or somewhere in Louisiana, to New Orleans. By the time she was eighteen, the gold rush to California was underway. Sometime later, she made her way to California and became a natural for the many brothels that sprang up.

As the number of women increased and the amount of gold decreased, Jule began looking for more opportunity. There was a silver strike in Nevada. She and many other working girls decided that all that glitters was not gold and turned to silver for their get-rich-quick schemes.

Virginia City, Nevada, is located about twenty miles southeast of Reno. It came into being when the Comstock Lode was discovered in 1859 on the eastern slope of Mount Davidson. The silver and gold boom drew miners and others seeking wealth. An estimated $300 billion was dug from the mines. Until 1876, the city grew. Office buildings sprang up. Gaming houses, luxurious brothels, and multi-storied hotels sprang from the wealth and opulence of the mining

town. And then came the decline. By 1879, little of the rich
veins of ore remained. The boom was over.

But the boom had not lasted as long for all the boomers
who came to Virginia City. At first, many men and a few
women rushed to Utah Territory. Because of the tremendous
increase in population, the area was soon Nevada Territory
and, in 1864, the State of Nevada. Julia Bulette was in Virginia City by that time; she had arrived in April 1863. Before
long she had established her business and was operating
from the northeast corner of Union and D Streets. To adver-
tise their profession, the courtesans placed either a red lantern outside the door or a red oil lamp in the window. The
love-for-money rooms where the women did business were
small and often called cribs. There was a bed, a small stove,
a window, and little else. Most of their belongings stayed
packed away in a trunk.

*This is "D" Street, Virginia City, Nevada, in the decade following Julia
Bulette's life and death there. These "houses" were commonly called
cribs. (Author's collection)*

Jule Bulette was a beauty compared to many of the girls working in Virginia City. She had a dark complexion. Her cheekbones were prominent and her lips were full and soft. Her long dark hair framed her face. She had a pleasant personality and a smile for everyone. Jule was described by those who knew her as "witty and vivacious." She had proposals of marriage, but many of them came on the whiskey breaths of customers. But if marriage was what she wanted from life, she never revealed it. She seemed content to practice her profession.

Strangely, Jule Bulette's reputation went far beyond that of a prostitute. One biographer put it this way: "She was generous to a fault, spent her money freely and bought costly jewelry and expensive clothes for herself." (Daniels, p. 27.) And if someone got down on his luck, or was ailing for some reason, Jule was prepared to help out.

On another occasion, an officer of the court spoke to a packed courtroom and said, "True, she was a woman of easy virtue, yet hundreds in this city have had cause to bless her name for her many acts of kindness and charity."

Those in the courtroom nodded in agreement. When they finished and order was restored, the District Attorney added, "That woman probably had more real, warm friends in this community than any other person."

Because of her charitable activities, the local fire department, Virginia Engine Company No. 1, elected her an honorary member. It was not a common honor. Fire companies were extremely important and useful in crowded, wooden communities in the West. But the firemen appreciated Jule's support and even crowned her "queen" of the fire company and paraded her through the festive streets of Virginia City. Those in the community that knew Jule well said of her: "A woman of easy virtue, but the best of her class."

That is the way Jule Bulette was; that is the way people felt about her. That is, almost all people. For in the early morning hours of Sunday, January 20, 1867, the end came for this kind and charitable woman.

Slowly, the facts of the death of Jule Bulette were made public. It was five a.m. and deathly still in the area of Union and D Streets in the early Sunday morning hours. A newspaper carrier paid little attention to anything except his route and the cold. It was not daylight and wouldn't be for a couple hours.

But then he heard a scream. He hesitated, then realizing where he was, thought nothing more of it until the afternoon.

There was only a single scream. No sounds of a struggle. The carrier stuffed the newspaper under the door and continued his delivery route.

It was nearing noon on Sunday when a female neighbor, Gertrude Holmes, came to Jule's tiny room. She and Jule often ate a late breakfast together. No one answered Gertie's knock on Jule's door, so she went around back and entered the unlocked rear entrance. Jule lay in her bed, a blanket pulled over her. She was on her left side and her feet were partially out of the bed.

It still did not occur to her friend that Jule was not asleep. But then she lifted the blanket. Jule was nude under the blanket. A pillow lay over her face. When the pillow was removed, there was a pool of blood. Gertie tried to shake her awake. She knew then that Jule was dead.

There were also indications that Jule was strangled to death. [Two doctors conducted an autopsy and concluded as much.] Fingernails had lacerated the skin on her neck. Her face was bloody, twisted, and frozen in a deadly grimace. Jule Bulette was dead, obviously murdered. A quick search of the premises revealed that several valuable items, including the trunk that she owned, had been stolen.

The Virginia City *Territorial Enterprise* newspaper expressed the dismay of the 20,000 citizens of Virginia City in a headline:

Horrible Murder—Woman Strangled
to Death in Her Bed
Blood-Curdling Tragedy in the Heart of the City

Chief of Police W.E. Edwards and his men collected additional information. A Chinaman, who kept house for Jule and tended the fire, had entered an hour or so earlier than Gertrude Holmes. He'd seen Jule in bed, but figured she was still asleep. He swept and brought in some wood before leaving.

After Gertie Holmes entered, a man named J.S. Kaneen observed the scene. He added that her clothes were on the floor next to the bed. There was, according to Kaneen, a short, cedar stick that was probably used to strike Jule about the head. The coroner's jury soon ruled, "We find the deceased was named Jule Bulette, a native of England, and that she came to her death by strangulation on the 20th day of January, 1867, by the hands of some person or persons unknown to this jury." (Daniels, p. 34.)

The newspaper reported Jule's murder was "the most cruel and outrageous and revolting murder ever committed in this city." It so shocked the community that all the mines were shut down on Monday for the funeral.

Rev. William M. Martin delivered the sermon at the three o'clock funeral ceremony on a stormy Monday afternoon. The funeral procession moved through the Virginia City streets to the Flowery Hill Cemetery. The Metropolitan Brass Band played somber music and sixty Virginia City firemen marched along, following the horse-drawn hearse.

Jule's grave was among ground reserved for firemen. When dirt had been thrown on the casket, the Brass Band mournfully began playing "The Girl I Left Behind Me." There was not a dry eye in the procession.

In the windswept cemetery, a plain board was hammered into place atop the grave. One word, JULE, was scrawled in black paint across the make-shift headstone.

Virginia City was vigilant for a while. Strangers eyed each other cautiously. So did friends. Somewhere, perhaps in their midst, was the ruthless killer who had choked the life out of this woman described in the local newspaper as "kindhearted, liberal, benevolent and charitable." (Daniels, p. 30.)

The days and weeks slipped by, and still Jule was on the minds of the lonely miners of Virginia City. And then an arrest was made. A Frenchman who called himself Milleian, was arrested for breaking into one of the Virginia City girls' cribs and attempting a robbery. He was forced to flee when the woman began screaming. After Milleian's arrest, the police investigated further and discovered he was in possession of Jule's trunk and several of her belongings. Other items of Jule's had been sold and had been returned and identified. Those who had the stolen goods came forward and identified Milleian as the one who had sold the items.

After questioning, the Frenchman was revealed to have several aliases. It was concluded that the most likely name of this mild mannered appearing fellow was Jean Marie a Villeian. About thirty-five years of age, police concluded that Villeian killed Jule for her jewelry.

The May 24, 1867, *Territorial Enterprise* spoke for those who knew Jule when it reported, "Nothing that has occurred of late has created so profound a sensation among all classes of citizens as the discovery of the murderer of Jule Bulette."

A month later, the trial of Villeian for the murder of Jule Bulette began. The jury trial began on June 26, and Villeian was found guilty of first degree murder. Villeian was sentenced on July 5, 1867. The courtroom and courthouse was packed, awaiting the Judge Richard Rising's decision. The judge ruled that Villeian would be hanged until dead.

It was April of 1868 before the court's order could be carried out. There were a number of appeals and rejections. A huge crowd gathered on April 27, 1868, to watch the hanging. There was some concern that Villeian would never live long enough to keep his date with the gallows. There seemed to be many around Virginia City whose idea it was to speed the execution along.

But on Monday, April 27, Villeian was hauled by carriage to the gallows located "above the Jewish Cemetery." Both the National Guard and forty sheriff's deputies escorted the condemned man. When Villeian was asked for his final words, he removed from his pocket a speech that he had carefully written in French. The gist of it was that he was being hanged because he didn't understand English.

When his speech was ended, the noose was slipped over his head. The platform made a thudding sound as it dropped out from under Villeian precisely as planned. The noose snapped his neck. He was pronounced dead two minutes later.

℘◯℘

A footnote: The respect that the 20,000 citizens of Virginia City provided Jule Bulette is noteworthy. In all the time from Jule's death in January 1867, through the investigation, the inquest, the funeral, the arrest, and the final execution of the convicted murderer, neither the legal documents nor news accounts ever refer to Jule Bulette as a prostitute. It was a final tribute, a final gesture, to this woman whom they all adored and respected.

Octavia Reeves

Most prostitutes, regardless of their color, were in some degree of trouble with their Western community. If law enforcement officials and the town board left them alone, the churches and the "upright" citizenry often protested. And, even if the women paid their taxes and their fines and didn't cause too much trouble for law enforcement, they still had the clientele to deal with. An unhappy patron sometimes would attack the prostitute. It was the brothel madam's job to protect her girls. Sometimes the madam had a boyfriend who helped her police the house. Generally, unless the crime was severe, the houses policed themselves. A policeman answering a complaint from a "respectable" citizen might drum up any number of charges to square the difficulty between the irate citizen and the prostitute. Charges might include drunkenness, swearing, public indecency, fighting, or any number of charges cited by the arresting policeman.

Octavia Reeves, an African-American living in Wyoming Territory, operated a "dive" and got her name in the newspaper on February 3, 1882. *The Cheyenne Sun* explained how, on Christmas night, there was a shooting. Those involved were "a Senegambian cyprian" named Georgie Cox and "a Jackleg gambler" named Matt Hall.

Hall was described as unscrupulous, dishonest and lacking professional standards, especially when he was fingering a deck of cards.

But if Hall was a jackleg gambler, what was Georgie Cox? The reporter said she was Senegambian and a cyprian. Senegambia is a region of West Africa in the area of the Senegal and Gambian Rivers. A cyprian? Another term for prostitute.

Octavia's house of ill fame employed African-American women. And Georgie Cox was one of them.

Matt Hall often frequented the Reeves establishment. He'd get drunk and his pickled tongue would get him in trouble as it did on the night in question.

On Christmas night, usually a depressing time for the women without characters like Matt Hall adding to it, Hall began raving about his gun. He said it had been stolen while he was at Miss Reeves establishment. The drunker he got, the more demanding he became. Where was his pistol? He was certain Reeves had it hidden away somewhere.

Reeves no doubt had seen enough drunks to know that a drunk with a gun was an especially dangerous thing. If she did have his revolver, she'd be a fool to turn it over to him in the condition he was in.

He pleaded with her to at least pay him for the gun. He knew she had it, he repeated. He grew angrier, slurring his words and moving closer to Octavia Reeves, his foul whiskey breath hanging like a cloud in the room. There was nothing she could do. He was too drunk to reason with.

When Hall had had enough, he reached under his coat and pulled out another pistol and waved it unsteadily under Octavia Reeves' nose. Again, he put his case to her, but added he'd have the lost pistol or her life. Which would it be? he asked, as he thumbed the hammer on the little hideout pistol.

Georgie Cox had taken this all in. Her boss, Octavia Reeves, was in serious trouble. Matt Hall was, indeed, "crazy from the effects of liquor," as one reporter put it. Still, Georgie bravely stepped between the little pistol and Octavia Reeves.

What Georgie heard next was a popping sound. Not ominous enough to be a killing blow, it seemed. But then, there was a fire in her breast and she felt faint.

The drunken Hall had shut his mouth for a moment. He looked at Georgie, then turned for the door. As he stumbled toward the door, he made it clear that if anyone tried to follow him, he'd kill them, and that included lawmen. In seconds, he was out the door, across the yard, and on the run.

It was up to Octavia Reeves and her other girls to get help. According to the newspaper, "As soon as the intelligence of the tragedy was brought to the knowledge of Sheriff Sharpless, he directed Deputy Fields to institute a search for the murderer's whereabouts and procure the apprehension at any cost." (*The Cheyenne Sun*, February 3, 1882.)

Meanwhile, Georgie Cox was shot, but not dead yet. And Deputy Fields was hot on the trail of Matteson Hall.

This was all hard luck for Octavia Reeves. The accounts of the shooting was all bad. Georgie was shot. Any dream Georgie had of prosperity and the good life were gone.

Octavia and the other African-American scarlet ladies were aware of their "place" in Cheyenne. There had been a reform movement in 1878 to rid Cheyenne of black prostitutes. The movement failed miserably. (Butler, p. 117.)

Reeves also had to withstand competition. The coming of the train began the boom that caused Cheyenne to grow and attract soiled doves and bawdy brothels. One of the most well-known of the scarlet ladies was Ida Hamilton. She arrived in 1878 and built the "biggest and most pretentious brothel ever to flourish in Wyoming." (*Cheyenne, City of Blue Sky*. Northridge, CA, Windsor Publications, Inc., 1988.)

Called "The House of Mirrors," the house dazzled clients with the floor-to-ceiling mirrors in the hallway. The house featured brick walls and sandstone lintels. Ida Hamilton brought in the most luxurious furniture she could find.

The grand opening was just as dazzling as the mirrored hallway. Miss Ida's plans called for engraved invitations to be sent out. They'd go only to the most prominent men living in the Cheyenne local area. Since there'd be an overflow of men, Ida decided to send to Denver for reinforcements— more women.

Miss Hamilton's house was such a success that some say she was able to retire after about seven years of sedulous service.

But this was not the way of Octavia Reeves. First, she had to take a back seat to the opulent Ida Hamilton. And life was seldom smooth for the likes of Octavia Reeves and her black sisters of joy.

So, with Georgie still clinging to life, Deputy Sheriff Fields continued on the trail of Matt Hall. For the first few days, Hall eluded Fields. Finally, after several more days, Fields caught sight of Hall on Lightning Creek near Fort Fetterman, 130 miles north of Cheyenne.

Fields, on spying his prey, kicked his mount into a gallop and set off to arrest Hall. But Hall was equally mounted, and the pursuit turned into a horse race for a while.

The exasperated Fields didn't seem to be gaining on Hall and his mount, so he decided on the expedient thing. Fields pulled his rifle from its scabbered, halted his mount, stepped down, and carefully placed a bullet in Hall's horse.

Hall tumbled from the falling mount and sat dazed long enough for Fields to remount and close on him. Like a hissing snake that has not yet made up its mind to strike, Hall threatened to shoot Deputy Fields. In the end, Fields subdued and restrained Hall and delivered him to the guard house at Fort Fetterman.

In the meantime, Georgie Cox died of the gunshot to the breast. Now it was a case of murder. All that was needed was to bring Hall to Cheyenne and try him for killing the woman.

There was no question, Hall was a scoundrel. He was described in the *Cheyenne Sun* as "a hard citizen, one of the bad men from Bitter Creek." He was no account.

Hall was "constantly on the outlook for trouble and ready with his gun at all times to accommodate an adversary or intimidate a foe upon the slightest provocation." It was "A Good Piece of Work" Deputy Fields had done, proclaimed a headline in the *Sun*. The reporter figured the public was in debt to Fields, "who with his life in his hand has been the medium through which so happy a deliverance has been accomplished." It was a proud and happy day in Cheyenne. The culprit Hall, a public enemy, was going to be brought to justice. He'd pay dearly for taking the life of Georgie Cox, the black woman. The cold, windy Cheyenne winter slipped away and soon it was time for Matteson Hall, the murderer of Georgie Cox to face justice.

The judge carefully "instructed the jury to remember that the character of the deceased should not alter their regard for the severity of the crime." Both sides presented their stories. The all-white jury listened and came back with a verdict of "Not Guilty."

It was a tough case to prosecute. How many all-white juries would convict a white man for killing a black prostitute? A white prostitute—perhaps. But certainly not a black one. Not in 1882 Cheyenne.

As for Matt Hall, it was recorded that he admitted that he was more concerned about being tried for horse theft than for killing a prostitute. Punishment, he noted, for stealing a horse was much more severe than for murdering Georgie Cox. (Butler, p. 111.)

In June, Octavia Reeves' name again appeared in the *Cheyenne Sun*. Dated Tuesday, June 6, 1882, a paragraph about Octavia made the paper:

"The woman Octavia Reeves, at whose dive Matteson Hall killed a woman named Cox, was before Judge Bean yesterday, accused of offending the peace and dignity of the community by keeping a house of notoriously bad repute. Her case was continued until today, and she was assigned quarters so constructed that she will doubtless be on hand when wanted by the courts."

Because of the bad publicity surrounding the unfortu nate murder of Georgie Cox, Octavia Reeves decided to move on. She settled in Laramie, Wyoming Territory, "with at least one of her Cheyenne co-workers, Hattie Turner." (Butler, p. 7.)

ഹോരു

BIBLIOGRAPHY

Adams, Judith. *Cheyenne, City of Blue Sky*. Northridge, CA, Windsor Publications, Inc., 1988.

Butler, Anne M.. *Daughters of Joy, Sisters of Misery: Prostitutes in the American West 1865-90*. Urbana, University of Illinois Press, 1987.

The Cheyenne (WY) *Sun*, February 3; June 6, 1882.

Daniels, Zeke. *The Life and Death of Julia Bulette: Queen of the Red Lights*. Virginia City, Nevada, Lamp Post, 1958.

The Virginia City (NV) *Territorial Enterprise* of January 22; May 24; June 26, 1867.

PART II

Lady Justice
Gone Awry

Elizabeth Taylor

And the Shame of Nebraska

A DOUBLE LYNCHING
A brother and sister hanged from a railroad bridge

"Fairfield, Neb., March 15. *Chicago Times* Special:

On January 8, 1885, six miles southwest of this place, a man named Roberts was killed by someone, supposed to be a boy named Taylor. The boy has since been confined in the county jail, awaiting trial. Eliza Taylor, mother of the boy, and her brother, Tom Jones, have been suspected as accessories in the killing of Roberts, as well as in many other crimes which have been committed in the neighborhood for the last ten years. The people of that vicinity have lived in terror of Lib Taylor and her gang.

"After the killing of Roberts a vigilance committee was organized for the protection of the people, and gave them thirty days notice to leave the country. Not taking heed to the warning, last night at 12 o'clock a mob of about fifty men surprised the house of Jones and, calling out Tom Jones and Mrs. Taylor hanged them to a bridge over the Little Blue. At half past 3 this afternoon the bodies were cut down by the coroner and an inquest held, with a verdict in accordance with the facts as stated."

The Omaha Bee, (Morning Edition), March 17, 1885

Many settlers in the American West had little more than a dream to accompany them to their homestead. Their vision of hard work and success sometimes worked out well. Start out with a little land, then buy more. Plant more crops, or run more cattle, or raise more horses. All of these accompanied by hard work brought prosperity.

Certainly, an invasion of locusts, a flood, drought, and even disease could cloud the dream. Even so, more hard work and ambition could correct those disasters.

But great tragedy was no stranger to the 19th Century United States any more than it is in the 20th, or will be in the 21st. Combine prejudice and ignorance and mix in with economic fears and woes, and tragic outcomes are frequent. And dreams die.

Still, when tragedy strikes, it does not always strike a family as mercilessly as it did the Jones-Taylor clan in southeast Nebraska in the 1870s and 1880s. Much of the cause of these burdensome problems was a woman with more than her share of enemies, a woman who might have been described in later years as being persnickety and not in her "place." And for those indiscretions, this wise, hardworking, attractive, and ambitious woman would pay dearly.

Born Elizabeth A. Jones, she was from Wales, but spoke, read, and understood English. Her father, John W. Jones, came to Missouri from Wales in 1868. The Jones family settled in Pettis County, northeast of Sedalia. The family consisted of Mr. Jones and his wife, Margaret, daughter Elizabeth, and three sons. Of those sons, Thomas was said to be the twin brother of Elizabeth. They were born about 1854 and were similar in looks, height, and stature. "Both were short, with good features, fair hair and light complexions." And both were said to "possess a drive and energy." (Williams, p. 10-11.) [Their brothers were William and John Jones.]

About 1872, the Joneses decided to move to Clay County, Nebraska. Going along with them was Elizabeth's new husband, James A. Taylor, also a Welshman. [Taylor was the son of Mrs. Martha Taylor of Lookout, Missouri, also in Pettis County. They had, according to Jean Williams, *The Lynching of Elizabeth Taylor*, p. 36, married in 1869.]

James and Elizabeth also had a new son, William, who went along. In Nebraska, on April 24, 1872, James Taylor filed on seventy-five acres in Spring Ranche Precinct in Clay County. They located about two miles east of the little community of Spring Ranche just off the Oregon Trail, near the Little Blue River. There was a larger town, Hastings, about fifteen miles northwest. And another son, John, was born in 1873. [A daughter, Maggie, was born about 1880.]

By 1880, swarms of Americans and Europeans were settling in Nebraska. The Europeans were "largely Welsh, Bohemian and Slovenes," (Drago, p. 156.) but others were coming from Austria and Canada.

There were differences among these people. Differences of politics, language, culture, and a Nebraska difference caused by some settlers wanting to farm and some settlers wanting to ranch.

For the Taylors, much of their trouble was over fences. And if the Taylors had heard that "Good fences make good neighbors," they'd have had quite a chuckle—in the form of "gallows humor," of course. Fences sometimes belonged to the Taylors, sometimes to their neighbors. It didn't matter who because, when mules, cattle or horses damaged fences, they had to be repaired.

It came to pass that when Taylor's mules, for example, knocked down a fence, the neighbor would draw up a bill for labor and materials. James Taylor would pay the bill, but Elizabeth didn't like this. She admonished her husband for not standing up to those who accused him. Now there we neighbors claiming that James purposely let his stock hogs tear down fences. How could a anyone tell whose mals had torn down the fence? Certainly, a mule wasn't going to confess. What if, Elizabeth wond fence was destroyed by the neighbor's cattle? Or what if the neighbor was tearing the fence down just to get some of the Taylor's money? Maybe that's what was happening.

Elizabeth encouraged husband James to not pay. Besides, she argued, when a neighbor's cattle tore down a fence, the neighbor was not always as eager to pay as James. James and Elizabeth had harsh words over this difference about the fences. She accused him of not standing up to these men and their unwillingness to pay.

It was a difficult time for the Taylors. The boys, Bill and John, were a handful. They contributed to a bout with depression that may have plagued Elizabeth much of her life. And when Maggie was born, Elizabeth had more cause to be depressed.

To help her through these trying times, James tried to soothe her and suggested that Elizabeth might want to invite her relatives to Nebraska. She could use the help. And when her relatives arrived and helped with the work, the Jones-Taylor settlement in Nebraska prospered.

Still, the fence problem would not go away. The more prosperous the livestock business became, the more trouble there would be over fences. It was a dilemma that boiled down to whether the profit from business was worth the loss of friendship.

But it was all perfectly legal, the business of repairing fences damaged by cattle. Actually, it was Texas cattle that made it necessary. Those great, longhorned herds were driven north from Texas, headed for Ogallala, Nebraska, and then on to Wyoming and Montana. In the beginning, the Nebraska Herd Law provided that restitution had to be ɔaid when Texas cattle damaged fences or crops. Later on, ɔ herd law meant to Nebraska folks that damage caused 'heir cattle had to be paid for. By the 1880s, most Ne- ɔns knew about this law and were prepared to use it.

'll, it aggravated Elizabeth. Certainly, she didn't like ɔhe had to pay for damage done by her cattle. But she insisted that she be paid promptly when someone else's cattle damaged her fences and crops. This attitude nearly developed into an obsession with her. If they wanted to play this silly game, she'd show them how. She'd collect immediately. No delays.

James Taylor spoke with her about this approach. He didn't like it. That was no concern to her. She had great ambition and wanted to prosper. Her husband, it became more and more apparent, did not share these goals. He may have even thought that proper women didn't act like this. He was dealing with an ambitious woman.

Soon, Elizabeth found that Nebraska had a "Married Woman's Property Tax." It provided that ownership of their property could be placed in her name. She could cut her own deals if he'd sign the papers. She talked to James. He signed without question. He turned over all rights of ownership to her. She'd run the place the best way that she saw fit. Soon, she was in control, driving hard bargains, and collecting debts. And if someone didn't pay up, she put pressure on them by threatening legal action. Everyone on the Little Blue knew of Elizabeth and her dealings.

This did not leave Elizabeth Taylor in the best light with men living in Clay County, Nebraska. They were not used to such independence in a woman. They didn't like how she was conducting business, but they didn't know what they could do about it. Rumors about Elizabeth and her ambition were fodder for the rumor mill. The combination of idle men, an ambitious woman, and gossip began to gnaw at her reputation.

And then in May 1882, there were more rumors. On May 27, Elizabeth's husband, James, became ill. He rode his horse toward the Little Blue River. A man stood fishing a short distance away. James slid down from his horse, walked to the river, dropped to the ground, put his face the water and began gulping. In seconds, he was dead fisherman hauled him out of the river, but it was too la

The family sent for the coroner. The coroner ruled that James had died of natural causes. Nothing at all unusual about his death. He'd been complaining of "feeling poorly and being troubled with stomach pains." (Williams, p. 16.)

But rumors were flying, Elizabeth must have killed James. Murdered him no doubt. How'd she do it? Simple. She bought Paris green—an insecticide—and dusted James and her potatoes.

Later that summer, Elizabeth's father, John W. Jones, became ill. They sent for the doctor and he found that the elder Jones had cancer. He was dying of it. No chance for recovery. In September 1882, John W. Jones died.

The men in the neighborhood stirred the old issues up again. She'd killed her husband in May. Now it was her father. Surely this woman would kill them all. She didn't need men. How did her father die? Did she poison him, too? Well, maybe not. After all, the doctor did find cancer.

For a while, especially since her husband had died, Elizabeth had found it necessary to hire help. The fence had to be watched, and the cattle had to be tended. In the meantime, Elizabeth collected debts by whatever means. She withheld mortgages, used the courts, and charged interest. She threw more fuel on already blazing mistrust and hate.

Newcomers to the Clay County area were warned about that Taylor woman. Her husband and father were dead and buried. Who'd be next? And in addition, it looked like she and her brother might just be stealing cattle. There was a new frame house that had recently gone up. The family had moved out of the old sod house. They were quite prosperous, it seemed. Maybe that was it. Maybe they were rustling cattle. That would explain their prosperity.

Elizabeth had sent for her twin brother, Thomas Jones. ̄e would share in the management of the property. Jones ̄ did some of the collecting on downed fences and put ̄ure on others. So together Elizabeth and Thomas were running the ranch. And soon they were managing over 1,000 acres.

Elizabeth's mother, children, and brother lived on the place. Thomas and Elizabeth shared the farm, worked together, and prospered even more. They hired Edward Proust to watch over their fences. The rumor makers backed off some, giving her room to get her life together. Still a pretty woman, a neighbor began having romantic thoughts about the widow. All in all, Elizabeth's life was returning to normal. No complaints; no rumors.

The amorous neighbor was a US-born Welshman named Rees T. Rees. He lived just across the road from the Taylors' sod house. And when she hitched up a team and went to town, townsmen got a good look at this handsome widow woman.

Women of Clay County were making note of this, too. They didn't like this threat to their own courting efforts. Certainly Rees or any other bachelor could be taken off the wedding block by this pleasant looking widow.

Born in Pennsylvania, Rees was the head of a household that included younger brothers and a sister. One of the brothers, Isaac, was crippled. Two years younger than Elizabeth, Rees was considered tall, dark, and handsome.

But if Elizabeth ever considered him as a mate, there is no evidence of it. She did date Rees, but when he suggested marriage, she rejected him. One of the most eligible bachelors in the area, Rees was too aggressive for Elizabeth. And in rejecting Rees, she made him angry. Who did she think she was to reject him? Rees was nearly as angry as the local unmarried women.

He traveled to Hastings, some twenty miles distant, and consulted with Judge William Gaslin. Rees consulted, not about his lack of luck in love, but about the mysteriou death of Elizabeth's husband. And what about all those m seen coming and going at Elizabeth's sod house? Shoul the judge look into this? Gaslin said no. There was no proof of foul play.

Other neighbors continued having troubles with Elizabeth and Tom. Edward Proust, while riding fence, ran on to two of neighbor John Llewelyn's sons. He caught them tearing down their father's fence. Proust warned the boys, then told his boss, Elizabeth Taylor. She confronted Llewelyn and he denied his sons had done anything wrong. His boys wouldn't do something like that. It was all Elizabeth's fault. Bitter, angry words flew back and forth between the two. If it was her fault, then Llewelyn should file a claim against her. She made it clear to him that she had a witness—Proust. No claim was filed. There were threats about filing claims for the downed fence, but nothing came of it.

During 1884, the Edwin Roberts family arrived in Nebraska from Wales. There were 85 acres bordering the Taylor ranch, and Elizabeth leased it to Roberts and they became friends. She even sold Roberts a team of horses and some hogs on credit. She saw to it that he need not pay anything until he had his fall crops harvested. It was a verbal agreement. No need for papers to be drawn up. They were friends.

But then Roberts heard the stories about the Taylors and their friendship cooled. It was frightening to the recent emigrants to hear these stories about their countrymen.

And it wasn't just Elizabeth and her brother that "caused" all this ruckus. Her sons, twelve-year-old William and eleven-year-old John, were into it from time to time. Not yet in their teens, the boys were considered bullies, ruffians, and "more than a bit mischievous." (Williams, pp. 20-21.) They even picked on Isaac Rees, Rees' crippled brother.

Then on October 12, 1884, her sons were caught tearing own fence at Llewelyn's. Llewelyn, Rees, and Austrian-rn Joseph Beyer tied up the boys and delivered them to r mother. Llewelyn had her this time. He was on his way ear out a complaint. This time, he had witnesses. Rees and Beyer witnessed it all. They left the boys with their mother and rode on.

When Elizabeth asked if they'd done it, they admitted to "getting even." Llewelyn had said terrible things about their mother. They had to get even. Jesse F. Eller, Grand Jury foreman, issued the indictment on October 24, 1884. It stated that the boys "did wantonly and maliciously lay down, prostrate, deface and injure a fence inclosing pasture land of John Llewelyn...." The Taylor boys were bound over for the May 1885 session of court. They were released on $200 bail into their mother's custody. (Williams, pp. 20-21.)

Elizabeth was trying to keep matters in hand. She and brother Tom let it be known that they were looking for hired help. They'd exchange room and board for work. There were Texas cowboys in the area that hired on. Some stayed a while, then moved on. Others were a little more permanent. It was just the kind of traffic in young men that fueled more rumors in Rees T. Rees' fertile mind. Maybe these young Texans were getting more than room and board?

And maybe not. Some of these young cowpokes had just disappeared. Vanished into thin air. Gone. Some had mail at the post office, but didn't pick it up. Rumors and more rumors fueled the flames of hatred.

Then on January 8, 1885, there was a deadly confrontation. Elizabeth Jones Taylor had a timber claim not far from her house on the Little Blue. [The *Hastings Gazette-Journal* of March 16, 1885, said the claim was on railroad land.] Since November, Joseph Beyer and Edwin Roberts had been helping themselves to wood from this claim. There was some question about the claim that left Beyer and Roberts thinking that they had a right to the wood. [One source says she brought suit against the two men over the claim.] (Swanson) So while the courts sorted it all out in their slow, deliberate way, Roberts and Beyer continued to cut and haul wood.

Elizabeth fumed over this. Her sons saw how irritated she became. And now, on January 8, here came the two me a team of horses and wagon rattling over the frozen ground, past Elizabeth's house toward the timber claim.

Elizabeth screamed at them, but they ignored her. Roberts merely clucked and whipped the team into a faster gait. Elizabeth was furious.

That afternoon, on Elizabeth's orders, an unnamed Texas cowboy that worked for Elizabeth hitched a team to a wagon and drove toward the timber claim. Elizabeth's sons, William and John, armed with shotguns rode along. Their mother wanted them to scare off Roberts. They met Beyer and Roberts returning, their struggling team, burdened with a load of logs piled on the wagon. The boys and Beyer and Roberts began yelling and waving their arms at each other. Roberts' team was nervous, hooves shuffling, clouds of hot breath rolling from the gasping animals. And then they bolted. Roberts held tightly to the reins, but Beyer was thrown from the wagon and stunned when he hit the ground.

Beyer, then heard a shot. The Roberts team and wagon broke into a labored run, headed out across the field. Soon, despite the heavy log load, they were at Rees T. Rees' house and he and Grant Bozarth and J.F. Eller waved them to a halt. Roberts laid sprawled over the logs, part of his face blown away by a shotgun blast.

William, who had snapped off the shotgun blast that killed Roberts, and John Taylor were arrested and jailed at Clay Center. Their mother tried to make bail, but bail was denied. Look what had happened while they were out on bail from the fence incident in October.

Their mother did manage to cut a deal with attorneys John M. Reagan and C.J. Dilworth. They'd defend the boys for $1,200. [One wonders what Reagan and Dilworth did to earn their money. Their clients, ages twelve and eleven, were jailed in Clay Center and were not brought to trial until sixteen months later. They were acquitted. The *Hastings Ga-*

zette-Journal (May 21, 1886.) reported, "What the evidence was against them we do not know."]

The cowboy driving the wagon was unidentified and was last seen repairing fence with Thomas Jones. He too disappeared. Whether he just rode on or met with disaster is not known, although Rees liked to think that he'd been killed and buried in a lonely grave. But there was never any evidence that this sort of thing had indeed occurred.

Tension mounted in both camps over these issues, real and imagined, and discussions over what to do was on everyone's mind. Elizabeth went to town and bought a new shotgun and ammunition.

Rees talked to G.W. Vangilder, John Llewelyn, David Bennett, and H.H. Hyde about running Elizabeth and her family from Spring Ranche Precinct.

Young Margaret Taylor was taken to her grandmother for safekeeping. Texas Bill Foster and N.C. Clark also stayed at the frame house. Thomas Jones and his sister lived at the sod house and checked the fences daily.

This activity caused the widow of Edwin Roberts considerable concern. Were they going to kill her next? As the days wore on, Mrs. Roberts grew more and more terrified at what might happen. She mentioned this to a neighbor and soon Rees T. Rees and John Llewelyn were advising Mrs. Roberts to take out a peace bond against Elizabeth and her brother. It was near the end of January 1885 when Thomas Jones and Elizabeth each posted a peace bond of $900. The Hastings attorneys, Reagan and Dilworth, acted as bondsmen.

It was early March when Rees called a secret meeting of Clay County farmers. On the night of March 5, over fifty men rode to the Mullen farm two miles east of Spring Ranch. They were quickly sworn to secrecy and someone in the group revealed that the plan was to escort Elizabeth and her brother Tom to the county line and exile them. Tell them to get going and keep on going. If they tried to come back, they'd be killed. That was the plan.

Many in the mob heard and understood for the first time what Rees, Llewelyn, and some others had in mind. But the strategy did not set well with all in the gathering. Several had come to the United States from Bohemia. They sensed something bad. This was the kind of uncivilized behavior for which they had fled old Europe. They wanted no part of this action and quietly spurred their horses into the night, heading home. [Swanson says the reason why so many of them didn't participate that night was because of a bright moon. They feared they'd be found out.] Whatever the reason, they disappeared into the night.

At the Taylor house, the night riders surrounded the frame house and called for all inside to exit. On this night, it happened that not only was Elizabeth's family in the house, but several cowboys were as well—Texas Bill Foster, Nat Clark, Bud Ferrell, and Nelson Cellery (Seely). [Some also add Luther Wiggins. See Denney.] They were ready for trouble. They'd give as much as they got.

There were shouts and threats and then, in the dark, from all four sides of the frame house, Tom Jones, his sister, and the cowboys snapped off a few rounds in the direction of the noisy invaders. It was too much excitement for Rees and his gang. They skeddadled, joining those in the original mob that sensed something not right about all this.

The next night, John Llewelyn's barn burned. Elizabeth had hired it burned. [Some say Tom burned the barn and that it was burned the second week of March.] (Swanson and Williams, p. 26.) And Elizabeth and the others made other plans to protect themselves. One of their first moves was to get out of the frame house for the relative security of the sod house and its thick, sod walls. They could not be too secure. Who could tell what the desperate, lawless riders would do the next time? Anything could happen.

It was about this time that someone slipped into Elizabeth's sod house and removed all their guns and ammunition—including a shotgun recently purchased in town. Enemies of the Taylors and Jones seemed to be everywhere.

With the hope that the outlaws would leave them alone, Elizabeth's ailing mother and young Maggie remained in the frame house. In daytime, it was obvious Elizabeth and the other adults were using the sod house. Certainly, they wanted that known.

Over the next several cold, March nights, they waited anxiously for what they figured was inevitable. Still, they had to take care of business, running the ranch, caring for their stock. And Elizabeth made a routine visit to Clay Center on Saturday, March 14. Just after midnight on March 15, the mounted men, between twenty-five and thirty-five this time, arrived again, their horse's hooves pounding over the frozen ground.

At the soddy, there were shouts for those in the cabin to come out. Thomas Jones yelled that they wouldn't do it. Commands to exit boomed out, warning that they'd drop dynamite down the chimney and blast them out if they didn't come out. That was a situation those in the sod house had not planned on. A few minutes later, those in the soddy decided.

The cowboys ducked through a sodhouse window first. There was John Farrell, Texas Bill Foster, Nat Clark, Nelson Cellery (sometimes Seely), and Luther Wiggins. They were met and their hands tied.

Tom Jones and Elizabeth, clad only in a nightgown, were next. The cowboys were led away to Rees' house and later released.

Could she have more clothes? she asked. Someone fetched a shawl. Her arms were tied to her sides. In the ten or so days since their first meeting, the vigilantes had changed their plans. Why not hang them?

Some in the mob had experience with lynchings. In March 1883, there had been a robbery and killing in Hastings. Cassius Millet was the victim. Everybody liked him. Three men were arrested, broken out of jail by a mob, and lynched.

No one protested. No one suggested that the mob was also breaking the law. The major difference between the Hastings hanging and the Taylor case was that there was more than circumstantial evidence against the men who murdered Millet.

Was Elizabeth Taylor really guilty of murder? Was she really a candidate for the gallows? Some in the mob recited a list of crimes they thought her guilty of. She denied them.

The mob marched Elizabeth and her brother Thomas to the thirty foot, half-moon iron and wood bridge over the Little Blue. They gathered halters from Elizabeth's corral and fashioned nooses from mule halters. At the bridge, about 100 yards from the sod house, the angry men threw ropes over the bridge stringers.

Thomas Jones and Elizabeth Taylor tried to size up the situation, but cold fear made it hard to reason. Jones began pleading for both their lives. He may have even reminded his murderers that he was a Master Mason of the Masonic Lodge at Hastings and had been for over a half-dozen years. But the pleas fell on deaf ears. Someone in the group gruffly called for Jones to make his peace with God.

The *Hastings Gazette-Journal* of March 16 reported: "At the bridge they told them now was the time to pray." Elizabeth gasped, choking back a sob, then cried out and fell to her knees. Her twin brother pleaded for mercy. And together, slowly, they began to recite the Lord's Prayer in their language, the Welsh language.

The irreverent onlookers forced Elizabeth and Tom to mount horses and led him into the sandy river bed under the bridge. The makeshift nooses were placed over their heads and someone fired a shot that caused the two horses to bolt and leave Elizabeth and Tom dangling and twisting in the cold night air.

Lynching was never a pretty thing. Usually, there was a great deal of disgust among observers. It was particularly disgusting to see Elizabeth Taylor dangling from a mule halter, her flimsy gown not quite hiding the body that civilized men identified with motherhood and life. A kerosene lantern thrust into her face revealed the stunned look of one who had died a violent death. All was silent in the cold, moonlit night.

The next morning, despite warnings against it, Nelson Cellery, one of the cowboys caught and released at Rees' house, returned to the bridge. His friends, Tom Jones and Elizabeth Taylor, were dead and he was overwhelmed. He recovered enough to spread the word. Some of the first to show up were Joseph Meehan, John Quinn, and Edward Young. Another source adds Ed Rollins. Coroner Jesse Eller and a four-man jury were there by early afternoon.

The coroner and his jury found the bodies hanging, twisting in a soft breeze. These men used their knives to cut through the mule harness and eased the stiffened bodies to the bank of the Little Blue.

The jurors ruled that Thomas and Elizabeth had been hanged "at the hands of persons unknown." (Drago, p. 108.)

The graveside services for Elizabeth and Thomas were secretly held the morning of March 16 at Spring Ranche Cemetery about a mile southwest of town. Their mother, Mrs. Margaret Jones, and Elizabeth's daughter, five-year-old Maggie, attended the pitiful ceremony. Also attending were William and John Jones, Elizabeth and Thomas' brothers who farmed in neighboring Nukholls County. Elizabeth's sons, William and John Taylor, were still in the wooden jail at Clay Center for the shooting of Roberts. They were yet to be arraigned.

Elizabeth and Thomas were buried in wooden coffins alongside Elizabeth's husband, James A. Taylor, and her father, John Jones. The undertaker at Fairfield had prepared the bodies. He also attended the funeral. [Mrs. Margaret Jones joined her husband on October 3, 1894. Markers were placed on all their graves that same year.] (Williams, p. 10.)

A preliminary examination was held in a crowded Clay Center courtroom. J.C. Kay, "a respected real estate man of Hastings," (Williams, p. 28.) had filed complaints and sworn out warrants for Rees T. Rees, G.W. Vangilder, John Llewelyn, David Bennett, and H.H. Hyde for the first-degree murder of Thomas Jones. [A sixth man named Barnhart was added to the list.](See *Omaha Bee*, March 31, 1885.)

The accused men armed themselves and holed up in the Harvard, Nebraska Metropolitan Hotel. The *Hastings Gazette-Journal* of March 25 reported, "It is stated that at least two of the very head leaders will, if such a thing can be done, stretch hemp." Fearing for their safety, they remained there until assured that they'd be taken to the Clay Center jail. Newspapers were calling these six "the ring leaders of the mob." (The *Hastings-Gazette Journal*, March 27, 1885.)

A few days later, the examination began. There had been a problem when the coroner's jury met. One witness, Nat C. Clark, "became too free with names of those he thought was in the mob." He was told to shut up since they figured his testimony wouldn't count for much. Although, "he had served one term of five years in the 'pen' for stealing horses and was known as a general hard character, he had been of late appearing pretty square." (The *Omaha Bee*, March 31, 1885.) He did not go before Judge Burnett.

The lynchers went before District Court Judge E.P. Burnett. The Clay Center courtroom was packed. Coroner Jesse Eller testified for the prosecution, as did Luther Wiggins and Elizabeth's mother, Mrs. Jones. They related what they knew. They heard the name Vangilder used, "but did not see him and did not know positively that it was him." Mrs. Jones claimed Vangilder came to her house about two hours after the hanging to borrow a lamp. "He then apologized for having disturbed them during the night and departed." The prosecution rested. The defense called no witnesses. There was argument by counsel and Judge Burnett summed up the evidence. The judge ruled that "the evidence was insufficient." (Williams, p. 34.) The prisoners were all discharged.

The courtroom exploded into applause and shouting, praising the verdict. One angry man screamed out to Attorney James Hayes who had prosecuted, that he ought to be tarred and feathered.

The *Omaha Bee* reporter summed up: "There is an opinion that nothing will be done till the meeting of the grand jury in May. The prosecution claimed to have other and strong evidence, and why they did not produce it and also other inmates of the house is severely criticised by many." (The *Omaha Bee*, March 31, 1885.)

Through all this, John and William Taylor remained in jail for the Roberts shooting in January 1885. J.C. Kay, a realtor who had done business with Elizabeth Taylor, was named administrator of the Taylor-Jones estate. Attorney Leslie G. Hurd was appointed guardian of all three of Elizabeth's children.

As for the boys, William and John, aged twelve and eleven at the time of the shooting, the *Hastings Gazette-Journal* of May 21, 1886 revealed their fate in Clay County: "The trial of the Taylor boys, William and John, charged with the murder of Roberts near Spring Ranche nearly two years ago, came off yesterday and they were acquitted.

"What the evidence was against them we do not know. The boys have been in jail all this time.

"The boys go into life under most unfavorable circumstances not of their own creation and beyond their control, but it is hoped they will grow into a manhood that will be respected."

Where was justice? There are letters to the newspapers that have come down from a century ago. The March 26

Hastings Gazette-Journal editor spoke of one that "made some good points in favor of the lynchers."

But Charles F. Manderson, a resident of Clay County at Sutton, took pen in hand, and wrote a letter that appeared March 30, 1885 in the *Omaha Daily Bee*. He wrote: "The hanging of Mrs. Taylor, however much it may attempt justification at the hands of the participants, was in itself cowardly, unprovoked and totally inexcusable. No matter what may have been the character of the woman in the past, no matter what may have been expected of her, good or bad, in the future, had she been permitted to live.

"Without process of law, without counsel to defend her, without judge or jury this woman has been heartlessly and ruthlessly executed for a crime in which no proof of her culpability has been shown."

As to Tom Jones' death, the letter continued, "Without warning, without provocation, without a friend near to whom he could look for consolation, he has been taken from his aged mother, whose support and comfort he was. The homestead he has so earnestly worked for and so faithfully earned and forced to give up his life, and by whom? By a mob composed of his neighbors, of men he frequently befriended and by them devilishly cold-blooded and cruelly hanged."

The *Daily Bee* added, "Clay County was a dangerous locality for any man to live in. He is liable any moment to be swung off into eternity from a bridge."

∽◯◯⬝

BIBLIOGRAPHY

Denney, James. "The Lynching of the Blue Valley Widow," *Sunday World-Herald Magazine of the Midlands*. The *Omaha World-Herald*, March 11, 1973. pp. 14-16.

Drago, Henry Sinclair. *Notorious Ladies*. NY, Dodd, Mead & Co., 1969.

The Hastings (NE) *Gazette-Journal,* March 16, 18, 23, 25, 26, 27, 1885; May 21, 1886.

The Omaha Bee, (Morning Edition), March 17, 1885.

The Omaha Bee, (Morning Edition), March 30, 31, 1885.

Swanson, Budington. "The Lynching of a Lady," *Real West.* No. 144, Vol. 19. March 1976.

Williams, Jean. *The Lynching of Elizabeth Taylor.* Santa Fe, NM, The Press of the Territorian, 1967.

Murder on the Sweetwater

The Watson-Averell Lynching

"A man and woman were the principals in a necktie
festival held up on the Sweetwater the other day."
Merris C. Barrow,
Bill Barlow's Budget,
August 2, 1889

The Great Plains states were filling up with a rolling tide
of farmers in the 1870s and early 1880s. Congress had
passed land acts for many decades, but most of them left
settlers confused about how the acts worked. The Land Act
of 1804 called for the buyer to purchase a minimum of 160
acres at a minimum of $1.64 per acre. Credit was extended
for four years.

The Land Act of 1820 reduced the minimum price to
$1.25 per acre and eliminated the credit system. Settlers
could lose the land under this plan if they did not pay
promptly. This cost of land seems cheap, but when taking
into consideration the cost of traveling west, purchasing
equipment, building a house, and just "getting by," it was
unreachable for many.

But then in 1862, the Homestead Act was passed. A settler could get free legal title to a quarter section, 160 acres,
by simply living on the land for a period of five years and
payment of a small fee. The newly opened Kansas-Nebraska
Territory attracted homesteading settlers first. Other Great
Plains territories followed.

But, there was a bit of a problem with the settlement. The act was passed to help draw people out of the East for settlement in the West. But the Civil War had created a shortage of workers. The government found it necessary to encourage immigrants from Asia and Europe by paying for part of their passage.

In Wyoming, by 1880, the Homestead Act had arrived. Still, there were only 457 farms. But in 1886 and 1887, iron rails stretched over Nebraska and into Wyoming, all the way to central Wyoming until they arrived at Douglas, a tiny tent city.

Douglas was named for former US Senator Stephen A. Douglas who had a good name and reputation. The town was also intent on building a good reputation. Even before a church was built, services were held in a local saloon. Participants that Sunday morning took off their hats and prayed around a card table substituting as an altar. When it was time to take a collection, no doubt some poker chips got mixed in with the ample alms.

By 1890, Wyoming had 2,125 farms. Understand now, Wyoming farmers were not exactly farmers. Sure, they filed for homesteads, but they had different motives. They harvested hay and began running cattle. And they began doing what the big cattle ranchers did. They let their tiny herds of cattle graze on land called public domain, land owned by the Federal government.

There was a difference though. The homesteader was sometimes considered foreign. He or she may have been from Kansas or Nebraska or some settled state back East. Leaving behind or selling their former homesteads, they now had their sights set on a Wyoming homestead.

The big cattle rancher also comprised a part of the population. They were often well-educated, wealthy, and well-connected. The government, whether territorial, state, or Federal, was always willing to help the prosperous cattle rancher—foreign or not. The poor, struggling homesteader seldom got a break from those prominent men. The rancher was always right; the homesteader was guilty until proven innocent.

[There are many examples of wealthy cattlemen being involved in the theft of horses and cattle. Seldom were they prosecuted or hanged.] (Helen Huntington Smith. *The War on Powder River*, pp. 71-75.)

Of course, it was the same kind of treatment big business was receiving from government in the growing industrial complex in the eastern United States. And the labor movement and the resulting conflicts in the eastern United States were little different than the way the homesteaders were being treated. So while the labor movement in the East was smelling gunsmoke and feeling the thud of the policeman's billy club, the homesteader in the West was suffering the same violence.

In the America of the late 1800s, "Justice for all" really meant justice for all those with money and power. It was a hard lesson to learn and even tougher to justify.

In the 1880s, one of the problems in Wyoming had to do with the large herds of the cattle barons and the small herds of the homesteaders. Their cattle mixed. The question: How to separate the cattle? How to tell to whose herd an unbranded calf belonged? They were difficult questions—questions that could get a man or a woman killed. (Smith, pp. 22-25.)

But this was not all going unnoticed. Many citizens were speaking out against what they considered wrong. Wyoming cattlemen, the big ranchers, had formed the Wyoming Stock Growers' Association (WSGA). Its purpose was to stop rustling. Punishment without benefit of the legal system was also a method used.

The action outside the law was disturbing to many, especially those who didn't have the money to buy themselves out of wrongdoings. Injustice, in whatever form it was found, was usually reported in local newspapers. And so

Wyoming citizenry had at least one place they could turn to protest mistreatment. From Laramie, Wyoming, a Democratic newspaper, the *Boomerang*, had its editorial say on shady Wyoming dealings. The *Boomerang* criticized the Wyoming Stock Growers' Association in December 1887, declaring that it "is stronger in Wyoming than the press, the courts or even the legislature." In addition, the paper quoted a "prominent" Wyoming citizen: "The custom of hanging a man who is suspected of stealing a $25 bronco and acquitting one who is known to have killed one or two men has ruled long enough."

The editor of the Republican *Cheyenne Sun* jumped on the bandwagon a day later: The WSGA is "a nuisance which ought to be regulated if not entirely suppressed." So, simply put, a war between the homesteaders and the big cattlemen was shaping up.

The big ranchers were grazing cattle on the same lands that the poor farmers had come west to develop. The question remained, were they willing to pay the price? Which might mean risking their lives.

To confuse the poor homesteader even more, he saw owners as mainly absentee. Many of the big ranchers were from aristocratic foreign-born families. It was the same aristocratic stock that these new pioneering homesteaders had fled Europe to escape.

Some of these homesteaders, looking at these owners and noticing that they had more cattle than they could count, decided to "requisition" a few head for food only, of course. In bad weather years, the homesteaders may even have taken more than a few head.

Lavish homes in Cheyenne and rumors of opulent dinners at the Cheyenne Club didn't help matters. From 1880 to 1890, the age-old war between rich and poor, new immigrants and old immigrants, south European immigrants and north European immigrants, was about to visit Wyoming.

This photo shows Ellen Watson and her first husband, William A. Pickell. They divorced.

(Photo courtesy of Lola M. VanWey, niece of Ellen Watson)

The erratic cattle industry had peaked economically in 1883. The grazing lands of Wyoming were overpopulated with cattle. In the years that followed, the weather played a trump card. Snow was heavy and the winters harsh in the mid-1880s. Some ranchers reported 90 percent losses. Never again would ranchers successfully turn their cattle out on open range and forget about them until roundup. Those days and ways were now past. Foreign investors suddenly realized that the cattle industry was, indeed, too good to be true.

The conversations at the Cheyenne Club, in the back rooms of saloons, even on the entrance steps of churches, often dealt with the hard times for cattlemen big and small, as well as homesteaders big and small. These were men and women struggling to achieve some sort of justice out of all of this. Too often, the definition of justice varied widely from person to person.

By the late 1880s in the Sweetwater Valley of Wyoming, the players were beginning to do what they believed they had to in order to survive. Violence erupted in the Sweetwater Valley. The "shot" was heard in Cheyenne, in Denver, in St. Louis, indeed, in Washington, D.C.

Ironically, the Sweetwater Valley was a beautiful place. On a day with warm sun, one could smell fresh mown hay and see herds of cattle grazing peacefully. It was nearly impossible to dream that murder and mayhem could ever disturb such peace and serenity. But in 1889, all was not well in Wyoming Territory's Sweetwater Valley.

Two of the players, James Averell and Ellen Liddy Watson, happened to be in the crosshairs. They apparently had no idea that there were "shooters" taking aim at them. They knew they had enemies, but not enemies ready and willing to commit mayhem.

And the "shooters?" All ranchers. John Henry Durbin—millionaire. Robert M. Galbraith—legislator and church leader. Albert John Bothwell—shrewd businessman. Tom Sun—former trapper. Robert B. Conner—charitable man. M. Ernest McLean—Durham dairyman.

None of the folks involved were natives of Wyoming. As a matter of fact, homesteader Ellen Liddy Watson was born in Canada. Her father was from Scotland, her mother from Ireland. She was born in 1861 in Bruce County, Ontario, about 200 miles northeast of Detroit. She was the oldest of ten children in this pioneer family of a dozen who had moved to Jewell County, Kansas, during 1877.

Ellen soon took a job as a housekeeper. A pretty, tall girl, Ellen stood five feet, eight inches tall. She was buxom, with blue eyes and auburn hair. She met and married William A. Pickell, but their relationship was not a good one. There was talk of cruelty, infidelity, and abuse, all aimed at Pickell. Some said they were incompatible. Yet, Pickell filed charges of desertion against Ellen and a divorce was granted on those grounds.

Ellen moved to Red Cloud, Nebraska, then to Denver, then to Cheyenne. She hired on as a cook and domestic at the Rawlins House, a room and boarding house in Rawlins, Wyoming. Her life was improving.

She took a job, no doubt to help ease hardships to her big family. And it was the kind of job that women in the 19th Century were expected to take if they were going to thumb their nose at an early marriage. She was courted, married, and abused, yet she had been divorced for deserting her husband.

In 1888, Ellen stepped out of character and finalized a claim on a homestead. It was not something that a woman did without having someone looking down his nose at her. This was getting into the sacred financial realm of men. Who did she think she was anyhow?

Jimmy Averell was born in 1851 in Canada as was Ellen. He was the youngest of seven children and when his father died, he moved to Wisconsin to live with his sister and her husband and to work in the sawmill. When he was twenty, he joined the U.S. Army and spent most of his two five-year enlistments in the West.

Averell was stationed around Buffalo, Wyoming. His service record was satisfactory. About the only difficulty from his Army days concerned a local tough named Charlie Johnson. At the time, Averell was stationed at Fort McKinney, outside Buffalo.

Averell and Johnson had had words strong enough to keep their anger stirred for several weeks. Johnson was in town on May 2, 1880, a Sunday, but he didn't have church on his mind. He drank some and then heard that the soldier, James Averell, was at Mrs. O'Dell's place.

Johnson stormed into O'Dell's and began addressing Averell in such a way to stir his blood. When the blustery Johnson progressed to cursing him, Averell reacted by unholstering his big Army revolver. Johnson sneered and called Averell "cowardly," and suggested that if Averell would put down the pistol, they'd fight. Averell, not quite 57, was not a big man; Johnson was a brute of a man.

Averell was no fool. He snapped off a shot from the big revolver. The shot went through the roof. He hoped Johnson would take heed and decide against any hasty action. He called to the drunken Johnson, stating that he didn't want to fight, but he'd not be called names either.

Over a dozen witnesses marveled at Johnson's lack of common sense and watched him step closer, making an even better target. The menacing Johnson leaned into his steps and kept going. Averell warned him again. But this time, he punctuated his warning with a bullet. He shot Johnson in the left leg. That blast spun Johnson around and Averell fired another shot that entered his back. Johnson died about a week later.

Charges were filed against Averell and a warrant was issued. After about a year, Averell was released. The court ruled that since Averell was in the Army, civil courts had no jurisdiction over the military. The Army would have to deal with him. Averell was never found guilty. The Army issued him an honorable discharge in June 1881.

Averell was discharged at Fort Fred Steele in Wyoming Territory and, after a few months, returned to Wisconsin. While there he married Sophia Jaeger and returned to Wyoming to make a claim under the Desert Land Act on a 160-acre homestead about fifty miles north of Rawlins in the Sweetwater Valley. Averell's new bride gave birth to a premature child in 1882. The child died, and a short time later, his wife died of "child bed fever." The bodies were returned to a family plot in Eureka, Wisconsin.

On March 11, 1884, Averell sold his homestead. By this time, he had filed for U.S. citizenship and was looking for another homestead. He filed papers again in July 1885. This new homestead was near the Sweetwater and he had some new ideas for it. He wanted to open a store and sell to neighboring settlers, ranchers, and travelers.

Averell set to work at this new homestead, constructing several buildings, fencing off a garden, and staying very busy building his road ranch along the Fort McKinney-Rawlins military road. His buildings stood along the Rawlins-to-Lander stage line road where it crossed the Oregon Trail about three miles east of Independence Rock. It was a good location with potential to bring Averell much wealth in the future. But, for one reason or the other, the potentials faded, one by one, until Averell hung his dreams only on the store. And the store did prosper—at first. But then debt built and creditors demanded payment. It was a struggle to keep ahead.

But then, there was a glimmer of hope. On June 29, 1886, Jim Averell, a vocal and active Democrat, was appointed postmaster at Sweetwater Post Office. He also was appointed justice of the peace. And, he was named notary public. Here was a new source of income.

These appointments did not set well with the local big ranchers, most of whom were members of the Republican Party. Already, Averell had stirred up some ranchers by irrigating across range land that was illegally fenced by Albert John Bothwell, a cattle rancher. Bothwell was not the kind of man to stand by when a threat to his making money got in the way. Averell may have been even more of a threat to Bothwell, since Averell knew how to survey land. With these skills, he could easily detect that Bothwell was committing fraud in his use of public lands. (Smith, p. 131.)

This wasn't an uncommon thing for a Wyoming rancher to to do in the 1880s. The rancher often made up his own rules as he went. Money and politics could always outdistance the law and justice in the race for water. But it wasn't Averell alone that was in this fight. Ellen Watson was also standing in the way. James Averell and Ellen Watson had met in February 1888, according to biographer/historian

George W. Hufsmith. (Hufsmith's *The Wyoming Lynching of Cattle Kate, 1889.*) They did not marry, since to do so would have limited the homesteads on which they could file. None the less, by the summer of 1889, Averell and Watson had holdings that added up to 640 acres, all of it in the middle of Federal pasture land and a hay meadow that Al Bothwell treated as his own.

There were complaints earlier about Averell, after he had been appointed justice of the peace. The ranchers evidently gave some thought to removing him. Wyoming Territorial Governor Thomas Goodnight, a Democrat like Averell, passed through the Sweetwater Valley to hear complaints. He heard that Averell was terrible and that his woman was "disreputable." Goodnight apparently did not agree with this judgment. He did not remove Averell from office.

As for Ella (Ellen) Watson being "disreputable," some remember her as being "very bright," neighborly, "fine looking," and hospitable. Similar descriptions of Averell have been brought down through history. Nathan Elledge knew Averell as a "quiet, easygoing, peaceable disposed person and had many friends among the cowboys and settlers."

The major differences seem to have been with Bothwell; the major problem seems to have been water. Averell's and Watson's legal claims cut off Horse Creek from Bothwell's cattle. Bothwell's response was to illegally fence some of Averell's and Watson's land.

John H. Fales, who was from the Sweetwater Valley, and knew Averell and Watson, wrote later, "It certainly wasn't any rustling operations of Averell's and Ella Watson's. Neither of them ever stole a cow." The problem was, pure and not so simple—water.

John Burke, a pioneer in the area, wrote that Averell's and Watson's claims "were in the center of a large section of country occupied by a cattle ranch, and the presence of squatters or settlers there was distasteful to the manager."

He added that Averell "was never accused of cattle stealing, never owned a single head." He added, "Ella Watson had received a few mavericks. These she had purchased from cowboys and ranchmen." (Hufsmith, pp. 149-50.)

Dr. Frank O. Filbey remembered Averell as a "pleasant little man...but a dangerous man if anyone tried to put anything over on him." Filbey would not buy the argument that Averell was rustling cattle.

And so, in an April 7, 1889, letter to the Casper *Weekly Mail*, Averell accused the large cattlemen of grabbing land illegally in the Sweetwater Valley. There had been some discussion about dividing Carbon County into two counties, and Averell wrote that he opposed that, since he also opposed the big cattle interests. With the Carbon County split, the cattlemen would have to strike new deals, mostly illegal, with the new county officials. Averell wrote that they, the big ranchers, were against "anything else that would settle and improve the country, or make it anything but a cow pasture for eastern speculators." In the letter, he more or less "attacked" Al Bothwell and Robert Galbraith directly, and the other cattlemen indirectly. "Is it not enough," Averell asked, "to excite one's prejudice to see the Sweetwater River owned, or claimed, for a distance of seventy-five miles from its mouth, by three or four men?" [This letter was also reprinted in the Rawlins newspaper, the *Carbon County Journal*.] Averell was striking at the very heart of the rancher's economy. For this, James Averell would pay with his life.

In the meantime, the first indications of the cattlemen's displeasure came in the form of small pieces of paper with drawings of a skull and crossbones. These were nailed on the appropriate doors. The Sweetwater Valley would not be so sweet during this summer of 1889.

Saturday, July 20, 1889, was a pleasant enough day. Ranchers John Henry Durbin, Robert M. Galbraith, Albert John Bothwell, Tom Sun, Robert B. Conner, and M. Ernest

McLean all rode out into a hay meadow, but they weren't enjoying the weather or the sweet Wyoming smells.

They talked some; they drank some. Bothwell emerged as the leader. He spoke the most, running on about Jim and Ellen rustling and branding cattle that belonged to the ranchers. Justice should be dealt out at the end of a noose, some agreed. It was not a unanimous decision, but the majority won out. Hang 'em.

It was just after the sun was at its highest when the ranchers rode up to the Watson cabin. They knew what they had to do. Their minds were made up.

Ellen was not home.

John L. DeCorey and eleven-year-old Gene Crowder were two wards of Ellen Watson. They paid for their keep by working around the homestead, taking care of the livestock, cutting and stacking hay—whatever was necessary. Ellen and John L. DeCorey, the older boy, had walked to the river where there was a Shoshoni encampment. Ellen fancied Indian beadwork, and on this day traded for a pair of moccasins. She was so happy with them that she slipped into them for the walk back home. It was a beautiful day.

Gene Crowder was "adopted." He had come to Ellen from a bad family situation. When the six rode up, young Crowder was trying to catch a pony. He ran out and yelled at them. Perhaps he sensed trouble. The boy ran back into the cabin, excited and not sure what to do.

It was such a pretty day. Ellen marveled at her new moccasins and she and John began the walk back to her cabin.

In the meantime, Ernie McLean rode out to find Ellen. He spotted her and the boy from a distance. They were walking at a leisurely pace, headed for the cabin. They'd be there in due time.

Bothwell told the others to take a look at Ellen's cattle. They were freshly branded. When Ellen and John got closer, they could see that there were problems. Two of the cattleman were tearing down her fence. The cattle were bawling, confused, and running out of the pasture. Ellen was waving her arms, screaming and trying to explain that she had a bill of sale for the cattle. Surely Bothwell knew that. Where was the owner and a bill of sale?

The owner was on the Oregon Trail, she explained. The bill of sale was in her bank at Rawlins. They laughed at her like the bullies they were. They had made up their mind. Nothing she said or did would change it. This was a man's world, and she was going to be taught that lesson.

DeCorey recognized the six men. They were ranchers from the valley. In particular, he had seen Bothwell here at Watson's place on several occasions, each time trying to get Watson to sell her homestead to him. (*Carbon County Journal,* August 3, 1889.)

Gene Crowder had seen what adults could do to each other. It scared him. With all the commotion outside, Gene Crowder decided to make a run for the store and Jim Averell. His pony stood bridled and tied to a fence post, right where he'd left him earlier. He looked for his moment, then ran to the pony, and headed for the hole in the fence.

Bothwell saw what was happening. He stopped the boy, jerked him off the pony, and ordered him to help with the cattle.

Bothwell then turned to Ellen and ordered her into the back seat of Tom Sun's new buggy. She hesitated. She wanted to know where they were taking her.

To Rawlins, one of them shouted, excited. Another shouted that they were taking her to Rawlins and the first train out of this country.

Couldn't she change into some proper clothes, she wondered aloud. Her face was wet with sweat. Bothwell glared and told her that "where she was going she wouldn't need any fancy clothes."

She ignored him and again asked if she could change clothes. Bothwell, impatient, warned that if she didn't shut up, he'd rope her here and "drag her to death" behind the buggy. He grabbed her and forced her into the buggy. Something bad was going to come of this.

Crowder remembered and told the Casper *Weekly Mail*, of July 26, 1889, "She got in then and we all started for Jim's. I tried to ride around the cattle and get ahead, but Bothwell took hold of my pony's bridle and made me stay with him." [This information was reprinted in the August 3, 1889 *Carbon County Journal*.]

John DeCorey added to this in the *Carbon County Journal*. "I started to follow them, but Bothwell pointed his gun at me and called me a bad name and told me to go to the house and not show up that day."

The five ranchers mounted and they rode toward Averell's road ranch about one and one-half miles away. Before they got to the road ranch, they met James Averell driving a Bain wagon headed for Casper. He had a load of empty beer bottles and was planning on getting them filled at the new Casper brewery. It was about 2:30 p.m. when Averell met up with Ellen and the angry ranchers.

Cooly, James Averell asked what the ranchers wanted. Bothwell lied and answered that they had a warrant for Averell's arrest.

Averell asked to see the warrant.

Bothwell and Conner raised their rifles and said the rifles would be "warrant enough." They ordered him into Tom Sun's wagon beside Ellen. With the Winchesters following his every move, Averell stepped out of his wagon and into Tom Sun's.

Bothwell rode ahead, leading the others out around Averell's store. He didn't want to arouse any suspicion or alert anyone to what they were up to.

[Unknown to the ranchers, this action was all closely observed through binoculars from a rooftop in the tiny community of Bothwell by the editor and assistant editor of the *Sweetwater Chief*. The editor, H.B. Fetz and J.N. Speer, his assistant, kept their mouths shut. Later testimony showed that they had seen everything.] (Rawlins, [WY] *Carbon County Journal*, November 2, 1889.)

Ralph Cole, Jim Averell's sister's boy, age 20, was tending the store while Averell went to Casper after the beer. With him was B. Frank Buchanan, also in his twenties. Several others were inside with Buchanan and Cole. It was cool inside out of the July sun.

Suddenly, DeCorey and Crowder came charging into the store. They had been let go. The handful of men in the road ranch listened as DeCorey and Crowder excitedly gasped for air and wove their tale of the six cattlemen and Averell and Watson. Once these loafers had heard the story, they quickly made their choices. Most weren't of a mind to get their spurs tangled up in this fight.

DeCorey and Crowder said that the ranchers were taking Jim and Ella "around the Rock." (Smith p. 124.) Cole went to Bothwell's for help, but found no one there. He returned to the store, but everyone was gone. He could do no more than wait.

Buchanan, the young cowboy, unlike the other loafers at Averell's, had reacted by buckling on his revolver and riding off in search of the cattlemen who had taken Jim and Ellen. Buchanan cut around Independence Rock and soon spotted the ranchers and their captives in the distance. He could hear them arguing. He decided to stay out of sight. The wagon bounced along through the brush. At the Sweetwater, the ranchers and their prisoners turned up the gravel riverbed and rode for two miles. Buchanan could still hear them continue the argument. At one time, Buchanan heard the cattlemen threaten to drown Jim and Ellen in the river.

Ellen, trying to be funny, pointed out that there wasn't much water in the river, not enough "to give a land hog a decent bath." (Hufsmith, p. 190.) No one laughed.

The men seemed to be moving aimlessly up the rocky river. Time and daylight were slipping away. Were they going to do it or not? What was going to happen next?

For some reason, the riders left the river bed and headed up Spring Creek Gulch. Huge boulders, sagebrush, and scrub timber cluttered the ravine. Finally the ranchers stopped and yanked Ellen and Jim from the back of the buggy and shoved them toward a 20-foot pitch pine tree. They had circled around in such a meandering way to come to this place only about two miles from Ellen's house.

Buchanan had been trailing them and, by now, had slipped to within 50 yards of the scene. Someone got a lariat around Averell's throat. He was yelling that they'd rustled no cattle and wouldn't be run out of the valley. But it was too late to argue. Even James Averell was coming to realize that. Things looked bad now. It might all end right here.

Ernie McLean was trying his best to get a rope over Ellen's head, but she was dodging and ducking. Could she please say a prayer, she begged. No. That was denied.

Finally, McLean managed to slip the rope over her head.

That did it. They had the rope over Averell's and Watson's heads. Buchanan had seen enough. He jerked his pistol and began slinging lead at the men. Buchanan remembered: "I opened fire on them but don't know whether I hit anyone or not." (Casper *Weekly Mail*, July 26, 1889 as cited in the *Carbon County Journal* of August 3.) John Durbin was hit in the hip and fell. The others lost interest in Jim and Ellen and went for their rifles. Who was this bushwhacker? Buchanan said later, "They turned and began shooting at me with Winchesters."

Buchanan knew he was too far off, but snapped off six shots, reloaded and commenced firing again. He had to try something, he figured. The bullets from the big Winchesters were whizzing all around him now.

But before Buchanan could retreat, he saw Bothwell run forward and shove Averell off the boulder. Ellen screamed. Jim's hands and feet weren't tied and he kicked furiously and tried to climb the rope.

Again Ellen screamed, but this time it was McLean who was shoving her off the rock into midair. She and Jim were suspended from the same limb and it bounced and bowed under their combined weight, but held. They grabbed at each other, each of them now drowning for air. Their bodies spun as they kicked and strangled, their eyes bulging, tongues finally out. Terrible, bloody, gurgling, animal sounds coming from them. Death finally theirs.

The shooting and shouting had stopped. A deadly lull hung over the hot rocks and brush. The cattlemen and Buchanan looked on in disgust. It was over. What else was there to do?

Brave, fearless Frank Buchanan did the only thing he could do. He told a newspaperman later, "I ran to my horse and rode to the ranch and told them Jim and Ella were hung."

Buchanan was outraged. He couldn't stay still. He rode on to Jim's store and reported there, too.

Armed with nothing but disbelief, Ralph Cole, Averell's nephew, rode to Sand Creek where there was a Justice of the Peace and Constable. Buchanan decided he'd ride to Casper and carry the terrible news there. He started out alone, a 55-mile ride in front of him. He was already exhausted, physically and mentally. No one offered to go with him to Casper, a town of about 300, to summon the sheriff. [He got lost in the night and stopped about 3 a.m., 25 miles from Averell's, and told his story again, this time to a homesteader named Tex Healey. (Smith, p. 125.) The rancher continued on to Casper, permitting Buchanan to rest up. Buchanan returned to Averell's store in time to hear two coffins being built.]

In the meantime, the six lynching cattlemen left the scene of the hanging, abandoning the bodies to twist in the late afternoon heat. As the story spread, a kind of dark sickness fell over the Sweetwater Valley. A woman. Hanged? For what?

When Deputy Sheriff Philip Watson at Casper heard the story, he rounded up a posse. This was about noon the day after the hangings. Coroner Dr. A.P. Haynes was sought, but not found, so a dentist was sworn in. The posse and dentist arrived about 2 a.m. Monday and the deputy insisted on retrieving the bodies at once. Another source claims the posse didn't get warrants signed and returned to the hanging place until Monday, 22 July. (Smith, p. 125.)

It took about an hour to reach the bodies in the moonlight. Frank Buchanan directed the posse to where he'd seen the hangings. Kerosene lanterns illuminated the dangling, bloated bodies, black protruding tongues, dead eyes staring. James Averell and Ellen Watson were cut down.

The first reporter on the scene, E.H. Kimball of the Douglas *Graphic*, described what he saw: "Hanging from the limb of a stunted pine growing on the summit of a cliff fronting the Sweetwater River, were the bodies of James Averell and Ella Watson. Side by side they swung, their arms touching each other, their tongues protruding and their faces swollen and discolored almost beyond recognition. Common cowboy lariats had been used and both had died by strangulation, neither having fallen over two feet. Still, a desperate struggle had taken place on the cliff, and both the man and woman had fought for their lives until the last." (From the *Carbon County Journal* of July 27. Smith, p. 295, note 7.)

Back at the ranch, the coroner's jury was sworn in and concluded that Jim and Ellen had been hanged by the six cattlemen. [Smith says this was on July 23, p. 125.] One large hole was dug for the two to be buried. It was southeast of the Averell's road ranch house. There was no sermon, no

SAN FRANCISCO: TUESDAY MORNING, JULY 23, 1889.

DANGLED FROM ONE TREE

Kate Maxwell, the Cattle Queen, and Her Male Partner Lynched.

THE WOMAN DIED "GAME."

Wyoming Stockmen Finally Rid the Country of a Pair of "Mavericks."

CATTLE KATE AND THE GAMBLERS

[Special to the EXAMINER.]

CHEYENNE (Wy. T.), July 22.—The strong limb of a big cottonwood tree in the shadow of Independence Row bore strange fruit this morning. A prairie breeze which wafted the sweet odor of modest flowers across the green plain swung to and fro the bodies of a man and woman, who had been lynched by stockmen the previous night. The discolored faces of the pair who had so long defied the officers of the law and plundered their neighbors, tongues which lolled from between swollen lips, and twisted limbs contorted by agony completed a ghastly picture.

The man and woman to whom justice had been so summarily meted out were George Averill, the Postmaster at Sweetwater, Carbon county, and the notorious "Cattle Kate" Maxwell, whose recovery of the winnings of "skin" gamblers from her men several months ago created such a sensation.

Very little in the San Francisco Daily Examiner *article was correct, but it was the first word that people outside of Wyoming got about the terrible lynchings. Now, over a century later, some of the same misinformation is being carried as truth.*

words from the Bible spoken over them. The graves were marked with two oak wagon wheels.

The names of the six cattlemen who killed Averell and Watson appeared in the inquest. There was no question about who had committed the first-degree murders. The *Carbon County Journal*, of July 27, 1889, named Durbin, Galbraith, Bothwell, Sun, Conner, and McLean. The Laramie *Boomerang* had already printed the names on July 24. (Mokler, p. 266.)

In the meantime, the six lynchers were apparently doing what they felt necessary to "justify" their murderous actions. Bothwell and Durbin rebranded Ellen's 41 head of cattle and shipped them by rail to Cheyenne. And a 10-word telegram sent from Rawlins to Cheyenne was picked up by George Henderson, a WSGA stock detective and ranch manager. Henderson was to deliver the brief message to the Cheyenne *Daily Leader*. [Smith, pp. 126-129; makes the argument that this was premeditated and that getting the news to the big papers was part of the smoke screen.] New York, Chicago, Omaha, Denver, San Francisco, and Laramie all picked up the sizzling story and printed it only hours after Averell and Watson had been cut down and buried in a common hole near the road ranch store. [The New York *World* of July 24, 1889, was one of the first Eastern newspapers to carry the Averell-Watson lynching. Smith, p. 295, note 9. The San Francisco *Daily Examiner* had the story on July 23.] Nearly all these accounts carried lies and misinformation. In most instances, the truth about what happened on the Sweetwater that day is still elusive. They wrote of "Cattle Kate," cattle rustling, the murderer Averell. And for the next century, the truth did not come out.

Edward Towse, a reporter for the Cheyenne *Daily Leader* wrote the first story about the lynchings. His story was in the Tuesday morning edition on July 23. He did a masterful job.

Merris Barrow, writing in his *Bill Butler's Budget*, on August 2, 1889, pointed out that Ed Towse took those ten words and "built an air castle eight sticks in height, crowned with a scare head. It was the finest bit of dime novel literature ever produced in these parts." He added, "Hardly a word of truth in it." Barrow and others acknowledged that the *Daily Leader* not only had the largest circulation in Wyoming Territory, but was "controlled" by the WSGA.

Towse had to use words that would paint Averell and Watson as guilty, especially Watson. It took a magic bag of tricks and lies to justify to anyone, rancher or not, that lynching was a fitting end for any woman, no matter how soiled.

Towse's *Daily Leader* article was full of lies. He wrote: "The man weakened but the woman cursed to the last." And "She was a holy terror." Based on the 10-word telegram sent by the cattlemen-lynchers, Towse concluded that "The thieving pair," as Towse called Averill and Watson, "were fearless maverickers. The female was the equal of any man on the range. Of robust physique, she was a daredevil in the saddle, handy with a six-shooter, and adept with the lariat and branding iron." Towse added, "She rode straddle, always had a vicious bronco for a mount and seemed never to tire of dashing across the range."

Among other things, Towse's story accused Averell of murdering *two men*. He wrote that Averell and Watson were hanged on the *Sweetwater* from a *cottonwood* tree. Perhaps worst of all, Towse confused Ellen Watson with Kate Maxwell, alias Cattle Kate, a faro dealer in Bessemer, Wyoming.

According to Smith (p. 129.), a Douglas, Wyoming reporter, picked up a "local rumor," and turned a case of mistaken identity into "Cattle Kate." Who was Cattle Kate? The rumor machine said that she held up a Faro dealer and stole his bank roll. She poisoned her husband. She shot a boy who had stolen her diamonds. She had stolen more cattle than any man in the West. And on and on the rumors and lies went, taking on a life of their own. At least one of the anti-cattlemen factions, the Laramie *Boomerang*, doubted there'd ever been a "Cattle Kate" Watson. (Smith, p. 129.)

[There was another woman with a similar name, Ella Wilson,who became confused in all this. She was involved in an 1884 shooting at Fetterman. The Cheyenne *Daily Sun* of September 2, 1884, described her as "a fair but frail young half-breed." At that time, Ellen Watson weighed in "at 165 pounds," was twenty-three, and stood five feet eight.] (Hufsmith, pp. 41-57.)

Towse concluded that the hangings were: "A case of life and death between honest men and cutthroat thieves." He wrote, "It is doubtful if any attempt will be made to punish the lynchers. They acted in self protection."

The other daily paper in Cheyenne, *The Sun*, more or less repeated the *Daily Leader* story. But a few days later, a more accurate story finally arrived in Cheyenne. This time, the *Sun* relied on someone other than Towse for information.

The *Sun* story told what happened. Tom Sun admitted the hanging as did Albert Bothwell. The four others were rounded up and surrendered in Rawlins to Carbon County Sheriff Frank Hadsell. [The wounded Durbin went to his home in Cheyenne to avoid arrest and let his wound heal.] There was a preliminary hearing in a Rawlins hotel room and each of the six was released to the other on $5,000 bail, despite the fact that first-degree murder was not bailable. No witnesses were called. The killers each signed the other's bond. Some would point to this as a mockery of justice. "Give bail for an unbailable offense," declared the August 2, 1889, Casper *Weekly Mail*.

The *Sun* reporter called Averell and Watson "worthless wretches" who "terrorized the whole region." He added, "It was not...a conflict between large stockmen and poor ranchmen, but a question of life and death between honest men and cutthroat thieves." (July 26, 1889, Cheyenne *Daily Sun*.)

The Cheyenne newspapers had done the best they could for the big cattlemen, but there was a need for more action. The Wyoming Stock Growers' Association got into the act with their crack team of attorneys Corlett, Lacey, Riner, and J.R. Dixon. The WSGA already had their newspapers in action, building a case against Averell and Watson in the minds of readers throughout Wyoming. It was time for the lawyers to make certain the guilty were proven innocent and the innocent proven guilty.

The first inquest had ruled that the six ranchers did the hanging. That didn't look good, not even in the courts that were under the thumb of the cattlemen. So, the county prosecutor ruled the inquest illegal. A new one was needed. The prosecutor, the Cheyenne *Daily Sun* reported on July 27, 1889, "was not, strictly speaking, an inquest."

For this inquest, most of the jury was not at or near the site of the lynchings. Ralph Cole, Averell's nephew, Frank Buchanan, and several others were in hiding in Casper. If they'd lynch someone in broad daylight and not get jailed for it, what would stop the killer ranchers? On August 24, Ralph Cole, age 21, died at the Averell ranch. It was assumed at the time that Mountain Fever killed him, although there were those who figured he'd been slowly poisoned. (Hufsmith, pp. 238-246; 257-264.)

When the second inquest results were made public, the August 1, 1889, *Sun* announced that the second inquest showed that "the verdict was that the parties came to their death by violence by persons unknown to the jury." The *Sun* could barely restrain its pleasure, but did editorialize, "This is more like it."

Slowly but surely, the remainder of the wild and woolly West was getting its hackles up. The open, admitted lynching of a woman was frowned upon, even by 19th century Wild West standards. There is "a crude chivalry which protects the most abandoned of women" [in the West], said the *Salt Lake Tribune* of July 27, 1889.

From Denver, Colorado, there was a mild scolding. The *Denver Republican* of July 27, 1889, said that there was enough evidence to convict the killers "unless public sentiment endorses and excuses the lynching of cattle thieves." By now, the cattlemen-lynchers were denying they'd ever admitted to the killings. In *Bill Barlow's Budget* of July 31, 1889, the editor and owner of the Douglas newspaper, Merris C. Barrow, planted his tongue firmly in cheek and wrote, "That settles it probably! Averell and Watson committed suicide, probably!"

There were many rumors and accusations rumbling around the West. Someone pointed out that Averell and Watson had lived together at some time, probably. The *Carbon County Journal* of August 3, responded, "It is reported that [Averell] lived with this woman Watson at one time and was not married to her, but if this is sufficient cause for mob law what a glorious field Wyoming presents for hanging parties."

Several Wyoming newspapers were into it now. The editor of the *Bessemer* (WY) *Journal* took a hard look at the evidence. He then apologized for his "hasty announcement." On August 1, 1889, he announced, "The trouble which led to the crime was not cattle stealing, but grew out of land difficulties."

The Casper *Weekly Mail* reported the next day that "personal feelings" is what caused the lynchings. The *Rock Springs Independent* called for justice. The *Carbon County Journal* spoke of the "highly colored accounts sent out by Cheyenne correspondents." John Friend, the *Journal* editor, added, "The Cheyenne papers are the only ones in the territory that condone the Sweetwater lynching. Averell...has always been spoken of as a peaceable, law abiding citizen."

The August 2, 1889, Casper *Weekly Mail's* James A. Casebeer, the editor, was still not done: "It is surprising that such leading papers as the Stock Journal, Cheyenne Sun and Leader should even hint that the crime is excusable." Case-

Purported photo of Ellen Watson. Notice unhooked throat latch, no visible saddle, and no stirrup. (Author's Collection)

beer continued, Averell "opposed the gobbling up of the public domain by individuals or corporations." Casebeer concluded that he "was personally acquainted with him (Averell) and knew that he expected serious trouble over land affairs in the valley."

Casebeer wrote, "James Averell was not a cattle thief, and if this business is sifted to the bottom it will be found that his death was caused because he opposed the gobbling up of the public domain by individuals or corporations."

The great majority in Wyoming Territory understood what was going on in Wyoming. The majority in the United States knew what was going on in Wyoming, as did the majority in Europe. And Merris Barrow had a prediction as to what *would* be going on in Wyoming: "The men who hung this man and woman will never be punished thereof. They have too much money and too many friends." (*Bill Barlow's Budget*, August 23, 1889.)

A Grand Jury met on October 14, 1889, at Rawlins. By October 26, when Frank Buchanan was to be present, Buchanan, according to some, forfeited his bond and fled the country.

Buchanan had earlier told the Casper *Weekly Mail*, "Averell had contested the land Connors [sic] was trying to hold. He had made Durbin some trouble on a final proof and kept Bothwell from fencing the whole Sweetwater valley." (This is cited in the *Carbon County Journal*, August 3, 1889.)

This is the same Frank Buchanan who rode out alone with a handgun to stop six men armed with Winchesters from murdering two people. The October 26, 1889, *Carbon County Journal* stated, "He is supposed to have been bribed to leave."

The case against the cattlemen flew out the window with the only eyewitness to the crime, Frank Buchanan. [Cole was already dead and Gene Crowder, according to some, had died with Bright's disease, a kidney disorder. (Hufsmith, p. 283.)] The lynchers were absolved.

No one knows what happened to Buchanan. The last anyone heard of him was in mid-September when he was spotted driving mules for the Niobrara Transportation Company. Some have him bribed and returning to the British Isles to finish out his life. At the other extreme, a skeleton found a few years later "about nine miles noth of Rawlins" was said to be Buchanan. Whatever happened to the fearless, courageous young man, it was to the cattlemen's advantage. The cattlemen who murdered Jim Averell and Ellen Watson were never tried. The deaths of Buchanan, Crowder, and Cole were never investigated. The people who had the most to gain from their deaths were never questioned. Justice was not only blind, but gagged as well. (Smith, p. 133.)

On the other hand, the cattlemen's cause seems to have been negatively affected. One WSGA member, approved of the lynching and said it came about because Averell occupied "land claimed either rightfully or wrongfully by more powerful interests." (Guernsey, Charles A. *Wyoming Cowboy Days*. NY, G.P. Putnam's Sons, 1936 as cited in Smith, p. 132.)

This sort of attitude may have influenced WSGA membership in the period. The WSGA claimed 400 members in 1885. By late 1888, there were 183 members. One 1890 source claims there were only 68 members of the Wyoming Stock Growers' Association.

Helena Huntington Smith, in her study called *The War on Powder River*, concluded, "The hanging was probably the most revolting crime in the entire annals of the West. There is something peculiarly offensive to a normal mind in the spectacle of a lynch mob of men strangling a woman, regardless of what she has done." (Smith, p. 121.) And the question remains, what had Ellen Watson done? What crime had she committed?

But perhaps the major problem in dealing with Watson and Averell is the problem of lies told well over a century ago. These lies have had a longer, more popular following, than the truth. The door was slammed on the truth by so many over a century ago, it has been most difficult to tell the true story of Ellen Watson and James Averell.

George W. Hufsmith's *The Wyoming Lynching of Cattle Kate, 1889* (Glendo, Wyoming, High Plains Press, 1993.) seems to have taken a major step in the direction of truth and honesty in the sad case of Ellen Watson and James Averell.

And what happened to the six cattlemen/lynchmen? Iowa-born Albert *Bothwell* was about thirty-four at the time of the lynching. He and Tom Sun became members of the WSGA later in 1889. Bothwell ranched for another twenty-five years. He had acquired Averell and Watson's homesteads by "legal" methods. He died in 1928 of Bright's disease.

Pennsylvanian Robert *Connor* was born in 1849. Has often been accused of rustling cattle in order to "get ahead." He returned to Pennsylvania and died in 1921.

John *Durbin*, born in 1842 in Pennsylvania, was in Wyoming early enough to become a charter member of the Wyoming Stock Growers' Association. He made millions, but sold out in 1891 and moved to Denver. He died in 1907.

English-born Robert *Galbraith* was born in 1844 and lived in Alton, Illinois, until age twenty-two. Involved in many moneymaking projects, Galbraith was a railroad worker, Wyoming Territorial legislator, church leader, and, from 1884, a rancher. When he sold out, he moved to Arkansas and became a banker. He died in Pine Bluff in 1939.

Ernest *McLean* was a small rancher, possibly from the Chicago area. Feeling some guilt over his role in the lynchings, he sold out and returned to the Chicago area not long after.

Tom *Sun* (Thomas de Beau Soleil), born in Vermont in 1846, was a trapper and railroad worker. Well-liked, he was an early settler in the Sweetwater Valley and lived there until his death in 1909.

As for Ellen and James, apparently no one came forward with Ellen's bill of sale for the cattle she claimed were hers. It was a dangerous time for the truth. Not many were prepared to step forward and defend Averell and Watson. after all, they were dead, gone from this life.

෨෬

BIBLIOGRAPHY

Bessemer (WY) *Journal*, August 1, 1889.

Bill Barlow's Budget (Douglas, WY) July 31, 1889; August 23, 1889.

Brown, Dee, and Martin Schmitt. *Trail Driving Days.* NY, Charles Scribner's Sons, 1952.

Butler, Anne M. *Daughters of Joy, Sisters of Misery.* Urbana, University of Illinois Press, 1985.

Carbon County Journal, (Rawlins, WY), July 27, 1889; August 3, 1889; November 2, 1889.

Casper *Weekly Mail*, February 13, 1889; July 26, 1889; August 2, 1889, August 30, 1889.

Cheyenne *Daily Leader*, Tuesday, July 23, 1889; August 29, 1889.

Cheyenne *Daily Sun*, September 2, 1884; July 25, 1889; July 26, 1889.

Chicago *Herald*, April 22, 1892.

DeBarthe, Joe. *Life and Adventures of Frank Grouard*, Norman, University of Oklahoma Press, 1958.

Denver Republican, July 27, 1889.

Hufsmith, George W. *The Wyoming Lynching of Cattle Kate, 1889*. Glendo, Wyoming, High Plains Press, 1993.

Laramie *Daily Boomerang*, December 7, 8, 9, 12, 1887; July 24, 1889.

Mercer, Asa Shinn. *The Banditti of the Plains, or the Cattlemen's Invasion of Wyoming*. Norman, Oklahoma University Press, 1954.

Mokler, Alfred James. *History of Natrona County, Wyoming 1888-1922*. Chicago, The Lakeside Press, 1923.

Moore, Austin L. *Souls and Saddlebags, Diaries and Correspondence*. Denver, CO, Big Mountain Press, 1962.

New York *World*, July 24, 1889.

Rock Springs (WY) *Independent*, August 2, 1889.

Rocky Mountain News, August 8, 1889.

Salt Lake Tribune, July 27, 1889.

San Francisco *Daily Examiner*, July 23, 1889.

Smith, Helen Huntington. *The War on Powder River*. NY, McGraw Hill Book Company, 1966.

PART III

The Female's Burden

Zerelda E. Cole James Simms Samuel
Jesse James' Mother

St. Louis *Daily Missouri Republican*, February 16, 1866.
"A most daring bank robbery and murder
was committed at Liberty, Clay County,
at 2 o'clock on the afternoon of the 13th."

Thus began Jesse and Frank James' dealings with banks and bankers. It was a bitter cold Tuesday when two men wearing Union soldier blue overcoats walked through the bank's front door, closing it quickly against the wind. This bank in northwestern Missouri was just twelve miles southwest of Kearney, the town just two miles from what was known as the Samuel's Place and is presently known as the James Farm.

The cashier of the Liberty, Missouri, Clay County Savings Association sat behind a desk. His name was Greenup Bird. His son William sat just to his left.

The overcoated customers, their heads pulled down in their coats' high collars, strode directly to the stove and seemed to be warming their hands. One of them spoke across the room and said he needed a bill changed. Young William Bird rose easily from his chair and took his station behind the cage where the Birds paid out and collected money. But at the window, William Bird found himself looking down the barrel of a big pistol.

The two bank robbers leaped to the countertop, their menacing revolvers waving in the air. Their demands came deadly quick: No noise! All the money! Be quick!

Wide-eyed William Bird was stunned by the events. He didn't move, Greenup Bird remembered later. The outlaws bounded down from the counter. One of the bandits struck the younger Bird in the back with a pistol and screamed, "Damn you be quick." He shoved the frightened, stumbling Bird to the open vault door.

Jesse Woodson James (Library of Congress)

In the vault, the robber quickly snatched a cotton wheat sack from under his coat. He told Bird he wanted the coins on the bottom shelf. They were special deposits of gold and silver and were in assorted rolls, bundles, and bags.

Outside the vault, the second bank robber had Greenup Bird in tow and was demanding that greenbacks and bonds and, apparently, revenue stamps be added to the wheat sack of loot. Be quick, he insisted.

The robber in the vault ordered William to stay there, and the robber with Greenup Bird insisted that the father should join his son in the vault. Greenup hesitated, but recalled, "He told me if I did not go in instantly, he would shoot me down. I went in."

The vault door was swung shut by the robbers, but it failed to latch. Using caution, the Birds opened the door, checked for the thieves and saw no one. The bankers dashed to a front window, and gave the alarm. So far, so good. (*Liberty Tribune*, February 16, 1939.)

But S.H. Holmes, walking along the board sidewalk, may have noticed something unusual. There were nearly two dozen men scattered strategically on the street, all standing by their horses.

George Wymore, a student at William Jewell College, was on the street near the bank, perhaps curious like Holmes. One of the two robbers from the bank suspected Wymore and Holmes were raising the alarm. With little consideration, the mounted outlaw snapped off a shot at Holmes and then at the bewildered Wymore. The slug hit Wymore. The shot was fatal.

Some in the gang were mounted now, their horses spinning and dancing in the streets. And then they were quirting and spurring their horses south out of town, their big pistols blazing as they headed toward the Missouri River ferry.

The sky was low and gray, and soon snow came on a high wind. It was a blinding, drifting snow and the posse from Liberty had no chance of tracking the gang any farther. The best opportunity to solve the robbery of the Liberty bank was gone. It was never solved.

Thus ended what author James Horan called "the first peacetime daylight robbery of an American bank." And so began a sixteen-year stretch in American History when the James Gang (often called the James-Younger Gang) robbed bank after bank and train after train. In many cases, they pulled off these holdups with the blessings of some citizens, those Americans disenchanted with big railroad companies, big business, and big money. [To this date, no one is certain who the two robbers in the Liberty bank were. Most conclude that eighteen-year-old Jesse was not along since he was still nursing Civil War wounds. Many figure it was twenty-three-year-old Frank James and twenty-two-year-old Thomas Coleman Younger, a guerrilla who Frank rode with during the war. Despite some evidence that Frank James was in Kentucky at the time of the robbery, historians and students of the James brothers have concluded that it was the group soon to be known as the James Gang that robbed the bank at Liberty. However, there has been no conclusive proof discovered in over 130 years since the Birds' turned over the $50,000-plus on Tuesday, February 13, 1866. A Jesse James museum is located on the site of the robbery at 104 East Franklin Street in Liberty.] (Richard Patterson, *Historical Atlas of the Outlaw West*, p. 87.)

The small farmers of Clay County, Missouri, who, along with other investors, lost, $57,072.64 in the robbery, did not take kindly to this theft. And they were angered by the death of young Mr. Wymore. A $2,000 reward was offered for the capture of the murdering scoundrels.

The *Daily Missouri Republican* concluded, "The determination to capture and hang the thieves is so universal that it is thought they cannot well escape." But they did escape. Always, they seemed to be one step ahead of law enforcement, private investigators, and the U.S. Army. Nevertheless, it was not until the robbery at Gallatin, Missouri, on December 7, 1869, that the law knew finally that it was the James boys who were robbing banks. From the remainder of 1869, through the 1870s, until Jesse was shot and killed in 1882, the outlaws rode a dangerous, bloody, murderous trail. Always, there was a reward—usually it was for the James boys, dead or alive.

Jesse and Frank James were the sons of Robert Sallee James and his wife Zerelda E. Cole James. Alexander Franklin, the oldest, was born in 1843. He had a brother, Robert R., who was born and died during 1845. Jesse Woodson James was born in 1847. The boys had a sister, Susan Lavenia. She was born in 1849.

Gold had been discovered at Sutter's Mill in California. The Reverend Mr. James, just over the age of forty, decided to rush to California.

Born in Logan County, Kentucky, in 1818, Robert Sallee James graduated from Georgetown College. [Later, in 1847, he earned a Master of Arts degree at Georgetown.] He married Zerelda E. Cole in December 1841. They had met while she was in a Catholic convent not far from where Robert attended school in Georgetown.

Confederate General Basil Wilson Duke attended college with Robert James. In a postwar interview, Duke recalled, "It was in 1840 that I attended...Georgetown...and Robert James...was one of my classmates."

He remembered, "At the time Robert James was twenty-one years of age, one of the oldest boys in the college, and he gave out that he had been sent there by the trustees of a church in Russellville, Ky. The boys at school looked upon James as a high-minded, honest fellow. He was a general favorite and much esteemed."

Duke added, "It was while he was preaching in one of the neighboring churches that he met Miss Cole, a bright and pretty orphan girl of sixteen. Her parents had left her a neat property valued at $10,000, a big sum in those days, and she was looked upon as a good catch for any one. James proved the lucky suitor, married her quietly, and a little later announced the fact to his classmates." (Horan, p. 30.)

In later years, a reporter for the *Louisville Courier Journal* interviewed Jesse Glass of Shelbyville, Kentucky. Glass said he was well-acquainted with Zerelda Cole "when she was a country girl living near Stamping Ground, in Scott county." The reporter wrote: "He represented her as a buxom country lass, with no over-nice sense of delicacy, brimming full of fun, a daring horsewoman, a good dancer and not afraid of the devil himself." (St. Louis *Missouri Republican*, April 6, 1882.)

Actually, Zerelda's father was dead, the victim of a horse accident, but her mother, Sallie, was alive. Sallie had married again to Robert Thomason, a widower, and Sallie, her new husband, and his six children left for Clay County,

Missouri. Zerelda's younger brother, Jesse Richard Cole, went with the Thomasons. Zerelda stayed in Kentucky. (Steele, *Jesse and Frank James: The Family History*, p. 42.)

The newlyweds, Robert and Zerelda, set out for Missouri a short time later in August 1842. Three years later, Robert bought a 275-acre farm near Kearney, Missouri.

In the few years that Reverend James lived in Missouri, he established three Baptist churches: New Hope, Pisgah, and Providence. James was also among the early organizers of nearby William Jewell College at Liberty. The Baptist college was founded in 1849.

But then something happened that changed Robert James. Gold was discovered in California. A gold mania reverberated from the mountains of California all across America, even to Europe, Africa, and Asia. The yellow metal that Native Americans claimed made white men crazy, was again taking its toll on sanity.

At the Rev. Robert James' 275-acre farm, there must have been some discussion of this. Did Rev. James try to explain to seven-year-old Frank, two-year-old Jesse, or seven-month-old Susan why he was leaving them? Did Zerelda send him to California with her blessings? She had a stormy disposition about her at times. Some called her "stern, domineering, aggressive, protective, and possessive." (Horan, p.61.) Was he tired of her? Or did he see California gold as the answer to all his problems? And there were other, nastier reasons cooked up by folks who thrived on rumors.

Whatever the reasons, it is unlikely that any will know for certain. The Reverend Mr. James saw to that. He died. [Letters written along the way to California, and after arrival do not contribute to the rumors, nor do they indicate that there was anything but the purest affection between Robert and Zerelda. In a letter written while on the trail to California, James tells Zerelda to "train up your children in the nurture and admonition of the Lord."] (Settle, p. 8.) Rev. James died on August 18, 1850 and was buried in an unmarked

*Zerelda Samuel, Jessie's mother.
(Photo courtesy the* National
Police Gazette, *April 29, 1882)*

grave. Asiatic cholera was sweeping across the continent that summer. Thousands came down with terrifying muscular cramps and vomiting. Their circulation slowed, eyes sank, and skin turned cold. Thousands died and were buried along the trails leading to California. Thousands more died in the gold camps of California. Somehow, Rev. James made it to California before the fever struck him down. He was just thirty-two years old.

Zerelda James and her three children were faced with the challenges of all broken families. Should they remain on the farm or sell it?

There was a great need for a man on the place. Should she marry? She was a young woman, only twenty-five years old.

In late September 1852, just over two years since her husband Robert died, Zerelda married a Clay County farmer and widower, Benjamin A. Simms. Simms, several years her senior, was not around for long. Tradition has it that the children were at the center of Simms and Zerelda splitting up. In Zerelda's eyes, he mistreated the children. Mr. Simms may have seen it differently. Perhaps the children mistreated him. Nevertheless, after a few months of marriage, they separated. A short time later, Simms was thrown by a disagreeable horse and killed. The accident was convenient. A divorce was avoided.

In September 1855, Zerelda married again. This time, she selected Reuben Samuel, a twenty-seven-year-old medical doctor. Zerelda was thirty and still an attractive woman. To this union were born Sarah Louisa (Sallie) 1858, John Thomas 1861, Fannie Quantrill 1863, and Archie Peyton 1866.

So Reuben and Zerelda settled down to tending the farm and raising their families. Until the outbreak of the Civil War, all seems to have gone along well for the James/Samuel family.

But Clay County, Missouri, was a turbulent place full of turbulent people when Jesse and Frank were becoming men and learning the ways of men. The Civil War didn't start until 1861 in most states. In nearby Kansas, killing, raiding, burning and looting had been going on since 1855. This violence and talk of violence spilled over into nearby Missouri. And if the James family escaped the anarchy, they certainly didn't escape the fear and hatred.

With the 1861 outbreak of war, a number of events began to unfold in Missouri. Guns and cannons were seized in Jackson County and in the Jameses' home county of Clay. There, a pro-Confederate group was formed. Eighteen-year-old Frank James was a member. Since his mother was decidedly a pro-South advocate, Zerelda Samuel no doubt influenced her son's feelings.

Lines were drawn in many areas of Missouri from the very beginning. Anyone sabotaging Union bridges, trains, or troops, would be shot. This order came from USA General Henry W. Halleck in December 1861. Just days later, Halleck proclaimed that guerrilla bands had no rights. Just months later, every man of military age was ordered to enroll in the Missouri state militia. Each man would be subject to call by the commander of the Union Department of Missouri.

Several incidents occurred in August 1863 that brought the controversy along the Missouri-Kansas border to a climax. A dilapidated three-story brick warehouse in Kansas

City, being used to hold enemies against the Union, collapsed. In this case, the prisoners were women, some related to the guerrillas riding with CSA Colonel William C. Quantrill. Four of the women were crushed to death. Another later died from her injuries.

General Orders No. 10 was issued by the Union Army. Under its provisions, anyone, or any family, assisting the guerrillas could be moved out of harm's way.

What appeared to be a Confederate response to that was William C. Quantrill's raid on Lawrence, Kansas. And the response to the Lawrence raid was still another Union order, General Orders No. 11. USA General Thomas Ewing's order called for the depopulation of Jackson, Cass, Clay and Vernon, counties—all in west-central Missouri. Americans living in Missouri, a Northern state, were forced to pack up and leave their homes. Impatient Union soldiers were accused of burning, looting, and killing. Many of the folks living in the targeted counties fled to Arkansas; others chose Nebraska. The order, designed to eliminate safe havens for pro-CSA guerrilla forces, is considered the most severe and dastardly military act directed at a civilian population during the Civil War.

Frank James was fighting for the South, a member of Quantrill's guerrillas, and his mother's sentiments were, naturally, with her oldest son. This made her suspect, and the Samuel farm was visited by a regiment of irate Union militia. The Samuels were interrogated. The militia tied a rope to a tree and around Dr. Samuel's neck to encourage him to answer their questions. They threatened to leave him there. Finally, when he was in danger of dying, they dropped him back to the ground. Dr. Samuel had apparently lost consciousness and the blood supply to his brain was cut off. Left disabled, he could no longer practice medicine on a regular basis.

Jesse, about age sixteen, was severely whipped by the militiamen. Mrs. Samuel was arrested a short time later and held at St. Joseph. That was during the summer of 1863. By the summer of 1864, Jesse had seen enough and had joined a band of guerrillas.

[Dr. Reuben Samuel's family and six others were banished to Rulo, Nebraska, in Richardson County, in early 1865. Jesse joined them there after having suffered his second, more serious battle wound. He did not heal well and begged to be taken nearer to home. He was transported to his Uncle John Mimms' boarding house north of Kansas City and was nursed back to health by his cousin, Zerelda Amanda Mimms. Before he left to return to the farm near Kearney, Jesse and Zerelda Mimms agreed that they would one day marry.] (Settle, p. 31.)

When the Civil War ended in 1865, the Jameses and Samuels eventually returned home. There were fields to plow and fences to mend. The family worked to get the farm back in shape.

But farming was not enough for the James brothers. It may have been too uneventful for them. Did someone suggest that robbing banks was exciting? After all, it was Yankee money they'd be stealing. It was Yankee money from big railroad companies, big business, and big money.

Zerelda E. Cole James Simms Samuel was proud of her boys. They had fought for what was right and just. They had fought the Yankees and should have won. But should they turn to robbing banks? There is no answer recorded by Zerelda, but it is known that she visited the bank at Liberty, Missouri, and may have left behind her sentiments. Historian James Horan wrote: "Three years after the robbery Mrs. Zerelda Samuel, mother of the James brothers, came into the bank and attempted to pay off a loan with revenue stamps taken in the robbery. It was reported that she became 'indignant' when she was forced to pay cash." (Horan, p. 36.)

Those who knew her claimed that Zerelda Samuel was always ready to explain how her boys were railroaded into a life of crime. Her version of the story told how they'd been

Confederate guerrillas and, even though the war was ended, the Yankees wanted revenge. She would repeat that story over and over to anyone who'd listen. (McGrane.)

None missed Zerelda Samuel's shrewdness when dealing with the enemies of her boys. Typical of her defense was an interview she did after an 1874 robbery. There was little question about whether she believed her sons guilty or not guilty. After a stage robbery on August 30, 1874, between Waverly and Carrollton, Missouri, across the river from Lexington, there was a great deal written about the James' being the culprits, along with others. When Zerelda James came to town, she had her work cut out for her. She tried to turn the media in favor of her sons. She agreed to an interview with the *Lexington Caucasian*. (October 17, 1874.)

The editor described Mrs. Samuel as "a tall, dignified lady, of about forty-eight years; graceful in carriage and gesture; calm and quiet in demeanor, with a ripple of fire now and then breaking through the placid surface; and of far more than ordinary intelligence and culture."

She talked about the boys' deceased father, the Rev. Robert James. She told of the injustice done the family by the late great war. She spoke of her incarceration at St. Joseph. She punctuated her remarks frequently with: "No mother ever had better sons, more affectionate, obedient, and dutiful." They were not the dastardly perpetrators of these awful crimes. Not her boys.

She told the same story after the July 7, 1876, Missouri Pacific Railroad robbery near Otterville in Cooper County, Missouri. Over the years, she was consistent. Her boys were the best, no question about it. They were not thieves, nor were they train robbers.

In the years that followed the 1866 Liberty robbery, several holdups occurred, but not all were immediately blamed on Frank or Jesse. It took a school boy's atlas to keep up with these robberies since the holdups were not only in Missouri, but also in Alabama, Kentucky, Iowa, Kansas, and Minnesota.

The *Lexington Caucasian* of October 31, 1866, reported the robbing of Alex. Mitchell & Co. in Lexington, Missouri. The four robbers were all young men under thirty-five. "They are, no doubt," the paper added, "Kansas red leg robbers."

The March 21, 1868, *Louisville Daily Courier* noted that in a robbery at Russellville, Kentucky, "The robbers were splendidly mounted and armed with Spencer rifles and navy revolvers. It was the most daring robbery on record." The March 22, 1868, *Nashville Banner,* had found that the two robbers stayed at a Russellville hotel and signed in as Thomas Colburn and Robert Boggs.

Still, the Jameses were not accused of any of these crimes until they made a fateful visit to Gallatin, Missouri. On December 7, 1869, two men robbed the Daviess County Savings Bank at Gallatin. The bank owner, Capt. John W. Sheets, was gunned down for no reason. The two outlaws snapped off shots at a fleeing bank clerk as well, but he was only wounded and made it to the door and sounded the alarm. Things were happening quickly. The two men ran to their horses, but one had trouble mounting. He was dragged down the street, his foot caught in the stirrup of the panicked horse. Finally, his foot came free of the stirrup and he climbed on behind his partner in crime and rode from town, the posse close behind.

The two robbers escaped, but the scared horse did not. When trailed, the unreliable horse headed directly to the Samuel farm in Clay County. The local deputy sheriff, John S. Thomason and his son Oscar, distant relatives of the Jameses joined the hunt. (Steele, *Jesse and Frank* etc., p. 80.)

Missouri Governor Joseph W. McClurg had opted to put more effort into the capture of the thieves. McClurg sweetened the pot. He sent a telegram on December 24, 1869, asking that the Jackson County sheriff put together a militia of 30 men and assist Clay County's Thomason in capturing or killing Frank James and Jesse James. Missouri would pay the actual expenses of the militia and $500 each for Jesse and Frank—dead or alive.

When Thomason's group arrived at the Samuel farm, Jesse and Frank, well-mounted, burst out of the barn and a chase ensued. Thomason's horse was up to the chase, jumping a fence and leaving the others behind. But when he reined his mount to a halt and dismounted to get a $500 shot at the James brothers, Jesse snapped off a shot that killed Thomason's horse and left him afoot.

They had a close call, but were still free. However, things were changing. Now they were hunted men. Lawmen were flying in every direction trying to catch the Jameses. Banks were robbed in Iowa, Kentucky, and Minnesota. There were trains robbed in Iowa, Missouri, and Kansas. The notorious brothers allegedly robbed a tourist stage in Kentucky and a government paymaster in Muscle Shoals, Alabama. And there were other banks, railroads, and stages that they were accused of robbing. Zerelda James Samuel said none of these crimes were committed by her sons. She and others collected affidavits that proved it, she claimed.

About halfway through this sixteen-year crime spree, the Pinkerton Detective Agency was hired by monied interests to put a halt to these outlaws, the Jameses. The Pinkertons planted informants and paid for information. And finally, one cold, wintry night on January 26, 1875, a raid was made on the Samuel farm.

Controversy has clouded information about the raid and its results for over a century. Some say the wily Pinkertons planned and led the botched foray; others blame it on railroad police. Still others accuse county law enforcement officials. Besides that, there has been speculation ever since that brutal, cold night as to what sort of explosive device was hurled through the Samuel house window. Was it a flare? Was it a bomb?

Whatever it was, it was destructive. The device exploded and flung shrapnel throughout the room. Jesse and Frank James' half-brother, eight-year-old Archie Peyton Samuel, was wounded in the side. Their mother Zerelda's right arm was so badly mangled that it required amputation. Dr. James V. Scruggs was called from Kearney to take care of Zerelda and little Archie. Before daybreak, the color ran out of little Archie's face and the quiet sobs of those grieving over him turned to wailing moans as the boy died. He was exactly six months shy of his ninth birthday.

The January 27, 1876, Coroner's Inquest revealed little: "Archie P. Samuel came to his death by means of a gunshot wound in the right side, inflicted by the bursting of a shell thrown in the house of Zerelda Samuel, by some unknown person or persons."

[The grand jury at its March meeting in Clay County indicted Allan Pinkerton and seven others for the murder of Archie Samuel. The indictment was continued on September 13, 1877, "a move which amounted to an involuntary acquittal."] (Yeatman, "Allan Pinkerton and the Raid on 'Castle James'," True West. pp. 16-23.)

The January 29, 1875, Kansas City Times reported that it was: "A posse of forty-six men, formed by Clay County Sheriff John S. Groom...." The Times, of course, was operated by Jesse's friend and supporter, John Newman Edwards. The deadly explosion had little effect on Zerelda Samuel. It turned her from a two fisted promoter to a one-fisted promoter of her sons.

Elsewhere, newspaper editors were prodded into action by the "bombing." If there was any doubt about the Jameses, it came into the open. Were these boys really innocent victims? And when did they fire-bomb a house or kill an innocent boy? Only the Pinkertons would do such a ghastly thing. After all, weren't they connected with big railroad companies, big business, and big money?

Sentiment built to pardon the James and Younger brothers following the bombing. Editorial writers in several Missouri newspapers fell in line. Among them were the St. Louis *Dispatch* and the Jefferson City (MO) *Daily Tribune*. They called for amnesty on the grounds that the young men had never had a chance. It was just what Zerelda Samuel had preached all along. She had told anybody that would listen.

Operating with a mother's full blown prejudice, Zerelda felt that her sons were unfairly picked on. Could she be held responsible for the criminal lives her sons lived?

The questions had often been asked: What if the Reverend Mr. James would have stayed home, not run off to California chasing after gold? What if the stepfathers would have treated the boys differently? And, what if there had not been a Civil War?

Author William A. Settle, Jr. studied the Jameses for over a quarter of a century. He concluded in *Jesse James Was His Name*, "There is no evidence to show that Frank and Jesse were any better or worse than normal boys of their time and circumstance." (Settle, p. 9.) This writing may reveal more truth than anything else. Remember, Clay County, Missouri, was a turbulent place full of turbulent people when Jesse and Frank were becoming men and learning the ways of men.

In addition to their mother, John Newman Edwards was one of the Jameses most ardent supporters. Edwards was a former adjutant to Confederate General Joseph O. (Jo) Shelby. Edwards, through his newspaper, the *Kansas City Times*, fanned the flames of Jesse's fame and let it be known that the killing, stealing, horse thieving, and terrorizing was justified. Edwards defended Jesse and his followers, explaining how the Jameses and their cohorts were driven into crime by an unforgiving government—the hated Yankees. To complicate matters, Edwards never permitted historical fact to get in the way of his glorification of Jesse. When Edwards took over the *Kansas City Times*, it became the "voice" and supporter of the James Gang. The *Times* also published letters written and sent to them by Jesse. And others, such as the St. Louis *Post Dispatch* followed suit. (Horan, pp. 35-36.)

Edwards, and others, were so successful in painting the rosy picture of Jesse and clan that even the President of the United States passed over a Missouri governor for a political appointment because the governor was involved in the killing of Jesse. [Thomas T. Crittenden was rejected by the Cleveland administration because "he had bargained with the Fords for the killing of Jesse James."] (Settle, p. 159.)

So why then didn't all riders with Quantrill and the other Confederate guerrillas, many who suffered injustices, become killers, bank robbers and thieves in the years following the Civil War? Why didn't Jesse and Frank's brother-in-law, Allen H. Parmer, ride the outlaw trail?

Parmer of Jackson County, Missouri, joined Quantrill at age fourteen, at the same time Frank James signed on. Parmer rode with the guerrillas until his surrender at Samuels Station, Kentucky, just northwest of Bardstown in Nelson County.

Parmer was accused of association with some of his outlaw friends and relatives, but there was little proof. And, of course, after his marriage, he was no longer in the area of northwest Missouri.

Born on May 6, 1848, Parmer was a teenager when he stopped at the James place during the Civil War. Susan Lavenia James, born November 25, 1849, was a young girl, but she and Parmer hit it off well, and by 1870 they were ready to wed.

Beautiful Susan, with light-colored hair, was two years younger than Jesse. They had been very close as youngsters growing up. There has been speculation that Jesse did not take it well when he heard his sister was marrying Parmer, a former guerrilla. Perhaps something had happened during the war to cause bad blood between the two. Perhaps Jesse's despondency over Susan's marriage to Parmer was a tale dreamed up by some long-gone myth maker.

Regardless, a May 6, 1882, *Kansas City Journal* article, claimed that Jesse put his foot down, saying there'd be no wedding. According to this story told by Dr. D.J. Simmons, Jesse was at his Uncle George B. Hite's place near Adairville, Kentucky. Dr. Simmons claimed in the *Journal* story, "In a fit of despondency, produced partly by his low state of health, and partly, as I afterward learned, by his bitter opposition to the prospective marriage of his sister Susie to Allen Parmer, whom she afterward married (Nov. 24, 1870). Jesse determined to commit suicide and, impelled by his impetuous nature, lost no time in his efforts at executing his desire."

He made the attempt with sixteen grains of morphine. He took it all at once. Frank sent to town for a physician. Dr. Simmons was called from Adairville. Simmons claimed that he found Jesse "apparently in the embrace of death, in a profound stupor, insensible to his surroundings, except under the influence of the strongest excitement; pulse slow, full and very forcible, and respiration of that heavy, slow and stertorous nature characteristic of opium poisoning." But, Simmons and the others were able to save Jesse.

There is other evidence that Jesse was merely suffering from old war wounds. As a result, he did what tens of thousands of Civil War wounded did. He took morphine to kill the pain. Sometimes, there were accidental overdoses.

The Parmer family, moved to the vicinity of Cane Hill, Arkansas, once Susan and Allen were married. Parmer's parents had moved to Arkansas following the war, so it seemed an ordinary thing to do.

Susan and Allen's son, Robert Archie, was born in 1874. Sometime that same year, Allen packed up his young family and moved to Grayson County, Texas. Susan taught school at Sherman, Texas, and had another baby, a girl, Flora.

By 1879, the Parmers were in Clay County, Texas. They lived at Boger Crossing near Henrietta. It was there that Zelma was born on December 19, 1879.

Their next stop was Wichita Falls, just across the county line in Wichita County, Texas. Here their world seemed to fall apart. Young Robert Archie drowned in the Wichita River. He was only nine-years-old. Then, Allen, Jr. was born in 1882, but died in 1885.

Another girl was born, Susan Kate, in 1885. And Feta was born in 1886. A stillborn child was born on March 2, 1889. His mother, Susan Lavenia James Parmer, died the next day. She was thirty-nine years old.

Susan had been a respected teacher and was one of the "eight original founders" of the Wichita Falls Baptist Church. She was buried beside her deceased children in Riverside Cemetery. Brother Frank attended the services.

Allen Parmer continued on with his life, taking a job as the general manager of the J. Stone Land and Cattle Company of nearby Archer City, Texas. In 1920, Allen and his new wife moved to Alpine, Texas. He died in 1927 while on a visit to Wichita Falls. (For more information, see Steele, *Jesse and Frank James* etc. and Steele, "Jesse James; Brother-in-law," *NOLA*.)

Late in the Civil War, Jesse had suffered a second wound and had made his way to Richardson County, Nebraska, to heal. [In August 1864, Jesse was wounded for the first time. He was wounded in the right side of his chest.] His mother, stepfather, and sister were there, having been exiled from northwest Missouri by Union order.

Jesse did not heal well and begged to be taken nearer to home. Some say that the wounded boy suspected that he might die and didn't want to die in a Northern state. He was just a short steamboat ride from Kansas City. He arrived in Harlem, a small community now within North Kansas City, Missouri, and moved into his Uncle John Mimms' boarding house. It was there that he was nursed back to health by his beautiful cousin, Zerelda Amanda (Zee) Mimms. It was there, in 1865, that Zee and Jesse knew in their hearts that some day they would marry.

Zerelda Amanda (Zee) Mimms James
Jesse James' Wife

They made a handsome couple, Jesse Woodson James and Zerelda Amanda Mimms James. Jesse was tall and slim. His dark hair neatly combed. His hazel eyes peered from under dark eyebrows. Zee was a pretty woman—with high cheekbones, beautiful eyes, and, even on her wedding day, a sad mouth.

Zerelda was also described by one author as "loving, gentle, fiercely loyal, and always trustworthy." She was a strong woman. (Horan, p. 61.)

Did she know how Jesse made his living? Apparently not. The *Kansas City Journal*, on April 4, 5, and 6, 1882, carried an interview with Charlie Ford, killer Bob Ford's brother. Charlie claimed he once asked Jesse if Zee knew what he did for a living. Jesse answered, "My wife doesn't know anything about my exploits and I never want her to."

"Jesse was very respectful of women," Ford recalled. "He was always ready to give them the time of day and would tip his hat. But when it came to telling anyone where he was hiding out, well, that was different." Ford added, "He didn't even tell his mother."

It was June 7, 1874, before the St. Louis *Dispatch* announced the April 24, 1874, wedding of Jesse James and Zerelda Mimms. The *Dispatch* revealed that their uncle, Reverend William James, Jesse's father's brother, performed the ceremony.

The James-Mimms wedding ceremony took place in Kearney, Missouri. Zee's sister, Lucy Mimms Browder, hosted the affair. The *Dispatch* got its information in June from Jesse as he waited in Galveston, Texas, for a boat leaving for Vera Cruz, Mexico. Jesse told the reporter, "About fifty of our mutual friends were present on the occasion and quite a noted Methodist minister performed the ceremonies. We had been engaged for nine years, and through good and evil report, and not withstanding the lies that had been told upon me and the crimes laid at my door, her devotion to me has never wavered for a moment. You can say that both of us married for love, and that there cannot be any sort of doubt about our marriage being a happy one."

The newsmen described the bride "with an elegant form, beautiful eyes, and a face that would be attractive in any assembly." Were Jesse and Zee really in Galveston? Did they leave the country? There is no proof either way. Jesse James stayed ahead of the law, ahead of those trying to find him and claim him as a hero or scoundrel, patriot or traitor, thief or "Robin Hood."

During 1875, Jesse (alias, John Davis "Dave" Howard) and Zee (alias, Josie Howard) settled in at Edgefield on the north bank of the Cumberland River across from Nashville, Tennessee. It was there that Jesse Edwards James was born on August 31, 1875. It is probable that the "Howards" may have moved to Tennessee as a result of the January 1875 bombing at the Samuel farm. (Yeatman, "Jesse James in Tennessee.")

In the meantime, back in Missouri prior to 1875, love was still in the air. Sometime, probably on June 6, 1874, Frank James eloped with Anna Ralston, the daughter of a wealthy Jackson County, Missouri, farmer. The *Kansas City Times*, August 16, 1876, announced that Frank James had married in Omaha, Nebraska.

The *Times* claimed that Samuel Ralston found out about the marriage when a posse rode up to his Jackson County

SCRIVER BLOCK, SCENE OF THE NORTHFIELD TRAGEDY.

Northfield, Minnesota, bank robbery site. (From the St. Paul Dispatch, *September 9, 1876).*

farmhouse looking for the thieves that robbed the Missouri Pacific Railroad at Otterville, Missouri, in July 1876. The posse looked Ralston squarely in the eye and informed him that they were looking for his son-in-law, Frank James. Others in the family knew this wedding had taken place, but Mr. Ralston hadn't heard about it until his house was surrounded by the posse.

Frank James visited the Ralston farm later. There were words between the new son-in-law and Anna's father. After a heated exchange, Frank James did the wise thing and retreated. Going up against the angry guns of an enraged posse was as much excitement as Frank cared to experience. This frustrated father-in-law was a completely different matter. He'd have to stay clear of him.

Frank and Anna joined Jesse and Zee in Nashville. They used the aliases Ben J. and Fannie Woodson. Zee claimed later that her family had traveled to Baltimore, Maryland, and remained there until after the infamous Northfield Minnesota Raid.

September 7, 1876, was one of the blackest days in the history of the James-Younger Gang. Some claim that Jesse and Frank wanted to leave Missouri for good, but needed one more big bank robbery. Then they'd leave and not come back. No one would ever find them. After all, they had been driven to this robbing, this outlaw way. It wasn't their fault.

So, in late August and early September 1876, Frank and Jesse James, Cole, Jim and Bob Younger, Clell Miller, William Stiles (alias, Bill Chadwell), and Sam Wells (alias, Charlie Pitts), all prepared for what was going to be a routine, normal "Hands up! Turn over your loot!" bank robbery. They hadn't robbed banks this far north. Minnesota was a long way from Missouri.

But what began as a routine holdup suddenly turned all wrong. Three of the James-Younger bunch had entered the First National Bank. Two more waited outside the door, guarding it. The other gang members were at the outskirts of town ready to make their getaway. Shots were fired inside the bank and outside in the street.

The townspeople of Northfield quickly armed themselves and turned the corner of Bridge Square and Division Street into a shooting gallery, with the James-Younger Gang being plunked like confused ducks on a perilous pond.

Suddenly, the air was full of hot lead, acrid gunsmoke, and shattering glass. The explosion of the Colts and Winchesters alerted the entire community. Amid the whining of bullets, some angry townsmen grabbed rocks and threw them at the bewildered bank robbers. There was no doubt about it, the citizens of Northfield were going to do whatever necessary to save their bank, their money.

One of the robbers in the street yelled through the door of the bank, "The game is up! Better get out, boys! They're killing all our men." [Actually, only Clell Miller and Bill Chadwell were killed at Northfield, but the air was so full of lead, most probably felt this might be their last day on earth.]

Finally, when the bank robbers were out of town and the gunsmoke had settled over Northfield, telegraph wires hummed with information. The newspapers joined in, announcing such things as: "Advise all over the state that all suspicious characters be watched."

Another item from Owatonna, Minnesota, on September 11 read: "A special train from Winona with 125 armed men passed here at 5 o'clock this evening, and the men are now at Waseca."

Another reported: "A force of twenty horsemen have just left here to patrol the bridges." It seemed the entire state was up in arms.

Fourteen days after the robbery and shooting at Northfield, a six-man posse led by Sheriff James Glispin surrounded the robbers in the town of Medalia, Minnesota, less than 150 miles from Northfield. Here Charlie Pitts was killed. Bob, Jim, and Cole Younger were all seriously wounded. The captives were taken to Faribault, Minnesota. Taken before a judge, they pleaded guilty and were sentenced to life in the prison at Stillwater. Somehow Jesse and Frank managed to elude the Minnesota posses.

Zee claimed that she and Jesse were still in Baltimore at the time of the Northfield fiasco. But by August 1877, Jesse and Zee (Dave and Josie Howard) were back in Tennessee living on a rented farm in Humphreys County about fifty-five miles west of Nashville.

Frank and Anna (Ben and Fannie Woodson) were farming on the Clarksville, Tennessee, Pike by early 1878. In February, Zee gave birth to twin sons. She named them Gould and Montgomery after the doctors that attended her. Neither child lived long. Anna and Frank's son, Robert Franklin James, was born that same February. Because Zee had lost her babies and because Anna couldn't produce milk, Zee fed the new baby. (Settle, p. 132.)

Through the remainder of 1878, all of 1879 and 1880, Jesse kept his family in or near Nashville. Mary Susan was born July 17, 1879. Their lives seemed to be taking on the appearance of ordinary family life. Jesse and Frank farmed some. They dealt in horses and did what was necessary to carry on a normal life and not appear suspicious.

Still, there was always the fear that some old gang member might appear on the horizon. And from time to time, a former member would show up in the area. One incident occurred in March 1881, when Bill Ryan (alias, Tom Hill) came around. Ryan was arrested north of Nashville and Frank and Jesse sent their families to safety in Kentucky, then rode across the Kentucky border themselves the next day. They couldn't take the chance that Ryan, under questioning, might reveal Jesse's whereabouts. It was not easy living a lie.

There were constant rumors of the death of both Frank and Jesse. Their mother would confirm it if asked.

George Shepherd, a one-eyed bank robber jailed for his role in the Russellville robbery, claimed he'd killed Jesse. Said it to the newspaper, reported in the *Kansas City Times*, November 4, 1879. Must have been so.

But just as quickly as someone stepped forward to claim he'd killed Jesse James, someone stepped forward and doubted it. In one case, it was none other than Robert A. Pinkerton, of the Pinkerton Detective Agency, who didn't believe it. He told the *Kansas City Times*, of November 20, 1879, "I consider Jesse James the worst man, without exception, in America." He concluded, "I don't believe Shepherd would dare to shoot at him." And Jesse's mother chimed in, agreeing with Pinkerton. She said she didn't believe Shepherd. It'd take a two-eyed man to kill Jesse, she argued. (Settle, p. 104.)

Politicians had always used the James Gang dilemma to promote themselves or attack their opponents. Law and order was always a major campaign issue. After all, the Jameses were a one-gang crime wave.

In the 1880 Missouri governor's election, Democrat Thomas Theodore Crittenden of Johnson County, a former Union general, vowed to get the James Gang. (St. Louis *Post Dispatch*, November 3, 1880.) In July 1881, the Jameses struck at Winston in Daviess County, sixty-five miles from Kansas City on the Rock Island & Pacific Railroad. It was the first outbreak in Missouri in nearly two years. Two men were killed in the robbery and Missouri seemed to turn against the Jameses. Editorials flowed in from all over the country criticizing Missouri for tolerating such savage behavior.

Some began to see that Missouri's nicknames, including the Robber State, were not good for the railroad business. It was certainly not good for Governor Crittenden's political life. He issued a proclamation to draw out an informer, some insider that would reveal to law enforcement officials the whereabouts of Jesse and Frank. Governor Crittenden did not call for the death of Jesse or Frank. Crittenden also asked the railroads for help.

Zerelda Samuel denied again that her sons were involved. They're both dead, she told the *Kansas City Times* of July 30, 1881.

Jesse reacted to this new "outburst" by the government by setting up warning flags and piling rocks and logs on the Chicago & Alton railroad tracks at Blue Cut in Jackson County, Missouri. That was on the night of September 7, 1881. The leader of the train robbers, the only one unmasked, declared through a full, black beard that he was Jesse James. It was the stuff of legend making.

But conditions were heating up. Before long, James Gang members would be arrested and questioned. Gov.

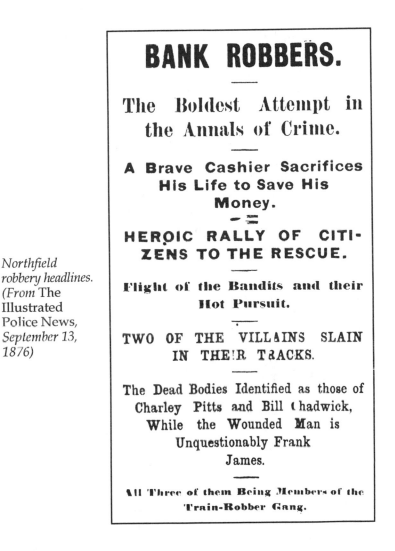

BANK ROBBERS.

The Boldest Attempt in the Annals of Crime.

A Brave Cashier Sacrifices His Life to Save His Money.

HEROIC RALLY OF CITIZENS TO THE RESCUE.

Flight of the Bandits and their Hot Pursuit.

TWO OF THE VILLAINS SLAIN IN THEIR TRACKS.

The Dead Bodies Identified as those of Charley Pitts and Bill Chadwick, While the Wounded Man is Unquestionably Frank James.

All Three of them Being Members of the Train-Robber Gang.

Northfield robbery headlines. (From The Illustrated Police News, *September 13, 1876)*

Crittenden changed his tactics somewhat by calling for the public to rise up against this lawlessness and keep after the outlaws until they were "either captured or exterminated." This "call to arms" was issued on September 14, 1882, in the Jefferson City (MO) *Peoples' Tribune*.

Charlie Ford claimed later that Jesse was living in St. Joseph, Missouri, during this period. For certain, Jesse and Zee were in St. Joseph from November 1881 to April 3, 1882. They were living there in March 1882, when Dick Liddel surrendered to the Clay County sheriff. Liddel, who had been associated with the Jameses since 1879, and was involved in some of the later robberies, was ready to tell all.

Jesse, now calling himself Thomas Howard, a horse dealer, was living at 1318 Lafayette, off 13th Street. The house at 1318 Lafayette was eventually moved and restored. It is now located at 12th and Penn Streets. (Patterson, p. 90.)

Then, on Monday, April 3, 1882, Zee, pretty and dressed in a calico dress that fit her well, was in the back of the house with her children, Jesse Edwards, age six, and Mary Susan, age two. Mary Susan was still in her high chair and little Jesse was toying with a coffee grinder. Zee was cleaning up after serving breakfast to her husband and the Ford brothers, Charles and Robert.

Bob Ford, the killer of Jesse James. (The National Police Gazette, *April 29, 1882)*

And then there was a horrible explosion from the next room. Did Zee suspect what had happened? Did someone accidentally fire a pistol? What happened?

Zee, her dark eyes wild with terror, rushed out of the back room and into the room where she found her husband, blood oozing from a wound in the back of his head. He was dead.

Zee screamed with horror and then as the realization of what had happened sunk in, her horror at Jesse's death turned to hatred of the

Ford brothers who had done the killing.

What if she would have had a gun? There is no evidence that indicates that Zee might have tried to avenge her dead husband.

When a reporter from the *St. Joseph Western News*, showed up, Zee didn't want to talk about the shooting. Slowly, she regained her composure. She told the reporter that the killers were named Johnson and that they had been living with the Jameses for a while. One was Charles, the other Robert. Charles, she told the *Western News* reporter, was a nephew. She'd never seen Robert until her husband, Thomas Howard, brought him home a while back.

She and Mr. Howard hadn't lived here long. They came out from Baltimore and had planned to buy a farm.

Was there a problem between the Johnsons and Mr. Howard? the reporter asked.

Zee shook her head, "Never. They have been always on friendly terms."

"Why did they do this deed?" the reporter asked.

Distraught, she replied, "That is more than I can tell. Oh, the rascals!"

Zee had been working in the kitchen all morning. Charlie helped her, but he walked into the front room some time between 8 and 9 o'clock. She heard a pistol roar and said, "Upon opening the door I discovered my husband lying in his own blood upon the floor.

"I ran to the front door as Charles was getting over the fence but Robert was standing in the front yard with a pistol in his right hand."

Charles and Robert Ford fled the scene, but returned later. It was not until Marshal Henry H. Craig arrived that the Fords admitted they were the killers. [Craig testified at the inquest that Bob Ford had been trying to kill Jesse for two months.] After a few minutes, the Fords gave themselves up to Craig, saying they'd killed Jesse James and now claimed the reward.

Reward! notice carried by newspapers after the Northfield robbery. (St. Paul Dispatch, September 23, 1876)

REWARD!

STATE OF MINNESOTA,
  EXECUTIVE DEPARTMENT,
    ST. PAUL, Sept. 12th, 1876. }

In lieu of the $1,500 reward heretofore offered by the State for the

Capture of the Outlaws

who recently committed murder and attempted the Bank robbery at Northfield, I hereby offer a Reward of

$1,000 EACH!

for the capture of the persons engaged in such murder and attempted robbery, the same to include and cover all liability of the State on account of such capture.

{ Great Seal) Given under my hand and
  of } the Great Seal of State the date
{ State.) above mentioned.
           J. S. PILLSBURY,
                Governor.
Attest:
  J. S. IRGENS,
      Secretary of State.   168

Marshal Craig was stunned. "My God," he gasped, "do you mean to tell us this is Jesse James?"

"Yes," answered the Fords. "This is Jesse James and we have killed him and don't deny it. We feel proud that we have killed a man who is known all over the world as the most notorious outlaw who ever lived."

When asked about this, Zee denied that her husband was Jesse James. A newspaperman crowded into the little room. He spoke up, "Mrs. Howard, it is said your name is not Howard but James and that you are the wife of Jesse James."

"I cannot help what they say. I have told you the truth."

The reporter replied, "The boys who killed your husband have come back and say your husband is Jesse James."

"Oh, is it possible they have come back? I can't believe it," she said, beginning to cry. She held onto her children and sobbed bitterly.

"Tell the truth," someone called out. She stood and walked into the room where her husband still lay on the floor. She looked around the room until she saw the killers, then screamed, "Why did you kill the one who had always befriended you?"

She left the room, the *Western News* reporter behind her. The reporter told her the killers were not mistaken, this was Jesse James.

Jesse's seven-year-old son responded, "God Almighty may strike me down if it is not my Pa."

The reporter said to her, "The boys outside say their names are Ford and not Johnson as you said."

"Do they say that? And what else do they say?" she snapped.

"That they killed him to get the reward money."

Holding her children close, she said, "I cannot shield them much longer. Even after they shot my husband who has been trying to live a peaceful life, I tried to withhold his name. But it is true. My husband is Jesse James and a kinder hearted and truer man to his family never lived."

Those in the room could hardly believe what they were hearing. Jesse James had been living among them for at least six months.

Zee James continued, "The deed is done and why should I keep quiet any longer? I will tell the truth. Charlie and Robert Ford are brothers and reside in Ray County, near

JESSE JAMES KILLED.

The Greatest Outlaw of All Ages
Shot to Death by a
Boy.

Robert Ford, His Cousin by Marriage, Kills Him in Cold
Blood,

For the Sake of the Glory and the
Forty Pieces of Silver
Involved.

The Remarkable Death of the Outlaw
in the Heart of St. Joe,
Missouri.

Passed in His Checks.
Special Dispatch to Daily Republican.
St. Joseph, April 3.—At 10 o'clock this morning
a rumor was rife that Jesse James, the notorious
outlaw, had been killed in his own house, at
Thirteenth and Lafayette streets, this city. Little

Denver Republican, *April 4, 1882.*

Richmond. They have been here with my husband and little did I think they would kill him."

She answered questions about recent robberies at Blue Cut and Winston, then said, "He was not half-bad as his enemies have reported. He has endeavored to lead an honest and peaceful life, but wherever he went he was hunted down by a lot of scoundrels who were not better than himself."

While the reporter shifted his interest to the Fords, Zee tried to keep people from carting off things that belonged to her husband. The house was packed. There was no control over the people of St. Joseph who rushed to the house, especially after they heard that Jesse James was the person murdered.

Once the *Western News* reporter had finished with the Fords, he turned back to Zee and observed, "The woman, his wife, is neat and rather a prepossessing lady, and bears the stamp of having been well brought up and surrounded by influences of a better and holier character than the reader would at first suppose."

The next day, Tuesday, April 4, Zee told the reporter: "I know Frank and Jesse have done wrong but they have not been guilty of all that has been charged. Jesse was as kind to me as he could be and for the children, he got everything they asked for.

"He...never told me where he intended to go but I had an idea of what he was doing."

Zee continued, giving her view of her husband, "The day he was shot he had been in the kitchen with me all morning until he went into the sitting room with the boys. I was sick at the time and he was helping me because it wasn't safe to hire a girl."

What about all the money from the robberies?

Zee responded, "There are some people who believe I have loads of money. That is not true. I have less than two hundred dollars."

[Later, Charlie Ford claimed Jesse had $1,500 or $1,600. There were some odds and ends of gold jewelry in the house. A gold ring was engraved "Jesse." There was a $1 gold coin made into a scarf pen with the initials "J.W.J."]

Zee James was apparently pressed for money. She later auctioned off household goods from the St. Joseph house. [Newspaperman John Newman Edwards actively raised several hundred dollars for the destitute Zee.] (Settle, p. 121.)

Zee told the St. Joseph reporter that they wanted to settle down, but officials wouldn't let them. They had lived in Nashville, Tennessee, for two years. Zee added, "If the officers had let Jesse alone we would have lived all right and I am sure Jesse would have been an honor to his country." (*St. Joseph Western News*, week of April 3, 1882.)

Missouri and the Midwest reacted with astonishment. Jesse James dead? Was the dead man really Jesse? Zee said so, but some others did not. Still, when Zerelda Samuel

SCENE OF THE MURDER

A sketch of the St. Joseph, Missouri, home of Jesse James, alias Mr. Howard. (From The National Police Gazette, *April 20, 1882)*

showed up the morning after the killing, she showed genuine grief.

And this time, there were a lot of folks who agreed that it was Jesse James and not Mr. Howard who died from the blast of a Smith & Wesson Schofield .45 on Monday, April 3, 1882, at the little white house in St. Joseph. (Yeatman, "The Guns of Jesse James," p. 20.) Others that verified Jesse's death were Clay County Sheriff James Timberlake, Kansas City Police Commissioner and Marshal, Henry H. Craig, and Jackson County Prosecutor William Wallace.

The two Zereldas, Jesse's wife and mother, identified the body. Dick Liddel's common-law wife said the body was Jesse's. Guerilla fighter, Captain Harrison Trow, was also certain that it was the body of Jesse James. The body had scars matching wounds known to be those of Jesse's. The left hand with the telltale missing middle finger tip and the war wounds were all in place. The puzzle was coming together. The dead man fit the lawmen's wanted posters.

Preparations were soon underway to haul Jesse's body back to Kearney. Already on April 5, Zee James received a telegram from a Cincinnati "preserving company." They offered $10,000 for the body and a percentage of what it would bring in when displayed over a couple years.

This telegram verified Zee and Zerelda's worst fears. The newspapers had been full of the assassination of President James Garfield over the past several months. The assassin, Charles Guiteau, was the target for some "preserving company" if it could be worked out. They'd preserve this notorious assassin then put him on public display for a fee. If Guiteau would draw a crowd, think what the famous outlaw, Jesse James, would draw.

At the inquest, it was revealed that Jesse was at his mother's farm about a week before his death. The Ford boys went along. Jesse's half brother, John T. Samuel, age twenty, had been shot at a dance in January. Jesse and the others came to visit their relative. Most figured young Samuel was going to die from the wound.

But the highlight of the inquest was when Zerelda and Zee, dressed in black, and the children entered the courtroom. The packed courtroom rose as one as Zerelda and Zee entered, young Jesse and little Susan nearly lost in the sea of humanity.

This drawing of the deceased Jesse James appeared on Frank Leslie's Illustrated Newspaper, *April 22, 1882.*

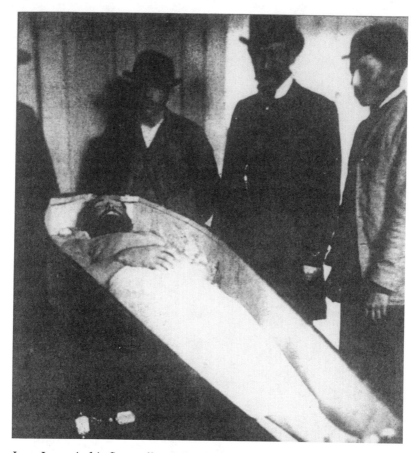

Jesse James in his first coffin. (Library of Congress)

It was not necessary for the two Zereldas to say much. Zerelda Samuel said the body was her son, Zee was her daughter-in-law, and the grandchildren were Jesse's. She had said everything. She rose to leave.

Across the room, Zee caught the eye of Dick Liddil. *The Kansas City Weekly Times*, April 6, 1882, claimed that Zee James called out, "Oh, Dick Little, you are the traitor who, with Bob Ford, killed Jesse and made me a widow. How dare you stand there and look me in the face, you traitor.

You did it, you did it, and before God, you traitor, punishment will come."

Mrs. Samuel spotted Liddil and began screaming at him, "Traitor—traitor—why did you kill my son?" [Another account says she screamed, "Traitor! Traitor! Traitor! God will send vengeance on you for this; you are the cause of all this! Oh, you villain!"] (Horan, 114.)

Liddil answered her, "Mrs. Samuel, I did not hurt him, I thought you knew who did it."

A half hour or so later, County Coroner James W. Heddens, M.D. and the six-man jury ruled that Jesse was shot in the head and killed by Robert Ford. "We the jury find that the deceased is Jesse James, and that he came to his death by a shot from a pistol in the hands of Robert Ford."

There was still controversy as Kansas City Police Commissioner Craig and Clay County Sheriff Timberlake argued over who was to get Jesse's body and guns. That issue was settled after Gov. Crittenden ordered that the body be released to Mrs. James "in the name of humanity" and the guns be kept for the State of Missouri. (Henry H. Crittenden, *The Crittenden Memoirs*, p. 188.)

Authorities were cautious, fearing that an attempt might be made to steal Jesse's body. After being kept under guard at Sidenfaden's Funeral Parlor, Jesse's body was returned to Kearney by special train and displayed at the Kearney House hotel. On April 6, he was laid out in a $500 galvanized iron casket.

At Kearney, it was almost a festive time with businesses and schools closed. An estimated 1,800 to 3,000 viewed the body before it was moved to Mt. Olivet Baptist Church. About 500 crammed into the church and heard the Reverend R. H. Jones of Lathrop, Missouri, read from Job 14:12; "Man that is born of a woman, is of few days, and full of trouble. He cometh forth like a flower, and is cut down; he fleeth also as a shadow, and continueth not." Kearney minister Rev. J. M. Martin preached the funeral sermon.

To help protect the body, Jesse's mother decided to bury Jesse in the yard at the farm. Neighbors dug a seven-foot-deep grave. A large procession from the funeral showed up to see the body interred.

Jesse's corpse was taken inside the Samuel house so that his wounded, bedfast half-brother John T. Samuel could view it for the final time. Young Samuel sat up in bed as they tilted the casket so that the boy could view Jesse's body.

Samuel was overcome with grief and sobbed, "Oh, oh, God! Oh, Jesse, that ever I should see you brought home this way."

Zerelda Samuel stepped from the cabin with Zee close behind. Zerelda was sobbing: "My heart is broke, my heart is broke; broke! broke! broke! Oh, my heart is broke! They have killed my son."

Frank James on trial.

(*The* National Police Gazette, *September 22, 1883*)

Jesse's wife called on God to avenge Jesse. She called Jesse her "good kind husband, who was slain by a cowardly murderer for money." Clinging to the coffin and laying her head on the glass that covered Jesse's face, "God will condemn and punish all who had a hand in murdering him for money." Standing and calling to no one in particular, she said, "Why did they kill him? Why did they take him away from me and my children? He would not harm them."

Mrs. Samuel, standing at the end of the coffin, added, "Yes, they killed him for money—for gold and greenbacks. It will do them no good. The officers of the law have done this. They have hired murderers to do it. God will judge them for it. I have no money. I want no money, I shall not judge them. I will leave that to God. If he can forgive them I can. Last week he was at my house," she said, referring to Jesse. "He said to me when he was going away: 'Mother, you may never see me again, but I am not as bad as they would make me out to be.'" (Hale, "The Resurrection of Jesse James.")

Zerelda and Zee's grief spilled over into the crowd of onlookers. They were a pitiful sight, Zee, the widowed mother of two small children, and Zerelda, who had seen enough grief and heartache for a lifetime. And neither would ever let go of their Jesse.

Zerelda saw to it that Jesse's body lay under a coffee bean tree in view of her kitchen window. Visitors were allowed at the grave and she displayed photos. By October 1882, she was charging twenty-five cents for this visit. (Settle p. 166.) She often related the story of injustice visited on her boys. She cursed the Fords and, through her tears, sold pebbles from Jesse's grave. The pebbles from the grave were also twenty-five cents.

From all across the United States, Zerelda received packets of flower seeds to be planted on the grave. There was a constant interest in Jesse James. As late as 1910, 25,000 visitors found their way to Kearney and out to the farm.

After two decades of watching Jesse's grave, Zerelda's health began to fail. She rented the farm and moved to town. In 1902, Jesse's body was also brought to town so that she could again keep an eye on the grave. Jesse was moved on a rainy, Sunday, June 29, 1902.

Jesse James, Jr., John T. Samuel, and, some sources say, Zach Laffoon and Zip Pollard, were involved in the removal of Jesse's body to Mt. Olivet, the Kearney Cemetery.

At the 1902 reburial, Jesse's body was placed in a new casket and returned to town. A reporter for the St. Louis *Post Dispatch* observed, "Not a sound was heard, not a funeral note, not a word was spoken at the grave during the twenty minutes required for carrying the coffin from the hearse, lowering it into the earth, shoveling in the clay and rounding off the mound."

But then, the reporter, Robertus Love, corrected himself: "Yes, there was one sound—just for a moment or two of the sobbing of Jesse's mother."

Anna James, Frank's wife. (The National Police Gazette, *September 23, 1883*)

Zee, Jesse's wife, lived in Kansas City and in Harlem (North Kansas City) after Jesse's death. The children received help from members of the family. Zee saw to it that she and the children lived frugally. And when her son Jesse needed a job, former Gov. Crittenden helped the boy find

one. Jesse, Jr. eventually had the cigar and confection con-
cession at the Jackson County Courthouse. [Jesse, Jr. ulti-
mately became a lawyer and practiced in Kansas City and
California.] It was a strange relationship, that of the ex-gov-
ernor and Jesse's son. It was Crittenden's actions that took
away the boy's father. It was Crittenden who gave the boy,
Jesse Edwards James, a chance at life. [When Jesse's wife
died, Crittenden was one of the pallbearers.]

Mary Susan had married the previous year to Henry
Lafayette Barr. She and her husband eventually lived at
Claybrook, a pre-Civil War plantation house, just across the
road from the James farm. Claybrook was her home until
1921. Mary Susan gave birth to three boys and a girl while
living at Claybrook.

On November 13, 1900, Zerelda Amanda Mimms James
died at her sister's home in Kansas City. Zee was 55 at the
time of her death.

Zerelda Samuel was to watch after her son's grave for
nearly one more decade. In February 1911, she was returning from a visit to her son and daughter-in-law, Frank and
Anna. They were living in Fletcher, Oklahoma. She had just
celebrated her 86th birthday and was, according to the *Kansas City Times*, of February 11, 1911, in failing health. She
died in Oklahoma aboard a St. Louis & San Francisco Pull-
man car. It was February 10, and Frank's wife, Anna, was
accompanying her back to Kansas City where she was to
meet Jesse, Jr. Her plans were to travel on to Excelsior
Springs, Missouri, where her son, John Samuel, resided.
Zerelda was buried beside Reuben Samuel in the Mt. Olivet
cemetery in Kearney. Samuel had died in a mental institu-
tion in St. Joseph, Missouri, on March 1, 1908.

Frank James had surrendered to Missouri Governor T.
T. Crittenden on October 5, 1882. Efforts to try him for various crimes fell short. He and Anna spent much of their time
on the farm at Fletcher, Oklahoma, but ended up back at the
farm near Kearney. (Henry Crittenden, p. 188.)

On February 15, 1915, Frank died of a stroke in the front room of the house on the James farm. His body was cremated and stored with the New England Deposit Company until Anna Ralston James' death on July 6, 1944. She was 91, blind and in ill health during her last years. She kept her word and never revealed the true story of Frank and Jesse James.

Frank's urn was buried alongside Anna's at Independence, Missouri, in the Hill Park Cemetery at 23rd Street and Rock Creek Road. (Hale.)

ℰℭ

ST. LOUIS POST DISPATCH, February 11, 1911

Mother Of Jesse And Frank James Dies On A Train

OKLAHOMA CITY, Feb. 11. Mrs. Zerelda Samuel, 86 years old, mother of Frank and Jesse James, died yesterday on a Frisco train near this city. She was on the way to Kansas City from the home of her son, Frank, who lives on a farm near Fletcher, Ok. She had been visiting him there for two months.

Mrs. Frank James, her daughter-in-law, was with her when she died.

Frank James and Jesse James Jr., a grandson, who lives in Kansas City, were notified of her death. Frank James is expected to go to Kansas City where the body was sent, to be buried near her old home.

Mrs. Samuels was born in Kentucky and was educated at a convent in Lexington. In 1841, she married the Rev. Robert James, a Baptist minister, and moved with him to Clay County, Mo., near the Kansas border. He went to California in 1849 and died there. In 1855 his widow married Dr. Reuben Samuels and until the opening of the Civil War they continued to live on the James farm.

During the war what was known as the "home guard" visited the house and their treatment of Dr. Samuel caused him to become insane. Some years later, when the boys had become famous as bandits, a visit from a detective caused the loss of Mrs. Samuels' arm. The men, in their anxiety to capture Jesse James threw a bomb into the house.

Mrs. Samuels used to charge visitors 25 cents admission to the Clay County homestead.

εϽ(Ϫ

ST. LOUIS GLOBE DEMOCRAT, November 14, 1900

MRS. ZERELDA JAMES IS DEAD

Widow of Missouri's Well-Known Bandit Passes Away

Special Dispatch to the *Globe Democrat.*

KANSAS CITY, MO., November 13. Mrs. Zerelda James, wife of Jesse James, the outlaw, and mother of Jesse James, Jr., died at her home, 3402 Tracy, this morning after an illness of ten months. In January of this year Mrs. James was attacked by the grip. Complications developed and she had been confined to her bed almost continuously since she first became ill. The funeral will be held tomorrow afternoon from the home. E.F. Swinney, R.L. Yeager, Frank P. Walsh, F.C. Farr, L.S. Banks and T.T. Crittenden will act as pallbearers, six of the most prominent business and professional men in Kansas City. Burial will be by the side of Jesse James at Kearney, Clay County, Mo.

Mrs. James had lived in Kansas City ever since her husband was slain in 1882 by Bob Ford. For some years she lived by doing sewing and other work for friends of the family. When Jesse, Jr., her son was 11, however, he went to work and since that time has been his mother's support. Mrs. James, Jesse and a daughter, Mary, lived in their own home, bought and paid for by Jesse before he was 21. Mrs. James was a member of the Methodist Church. She was a good, consistent Christian woman. When she came to this city to live she joined a Methodist church and kept up her membership to the day of her death. She sent her boy and girl regularly to Sunday school. It was Mrs. James who prevented her boy from going upon the stage, and she tried to keep him from posing as the son of a bandit. She hated to be looked upon simply as the widow of a bandit. She kept the relics of her husband's bandit career in the background and tried to put the memory of it there, too. She refused large offers from publishers of sensational books for a life of Jesse James.

εϽ(Ϫ

Bibliography

Coroner's Inquest (Archie P. Samuel); Clay County, Missouri. January 27, 1875.

Crittenden, Governor Thomas Theodore. "Messages and Proclamations on Outlawry in Missouri and the Breakup of the James-Younger Gang, 1883," *Messages and Proclamations of the Governors of the State of Missouri*. Vol. VI, pp. 303-308. The State Historical Society of Missouri.

Crittenden, Henry Houston. *The Crittenden Memoirs*, NY, G.P. Putnam's Sons, 1936.

Gilbert, Joan. "Zerelda Samuel: Mother of A Legend," *Ozarks Mountaineer*. December 1993. Vol. 41, No. 10 & 11. pp. 52-54.

Hale, Donald R. "The Resurrection of Jesse James," *Quarterly of the National Association and Center for Outlaw and Lawmen History*. Vol. V, Number 3, April 1980.

Horan, James D. *The Authentic Wild West: The Outlaws*. NY, Crown Publishers, Inc., 1977.

Huntington, George. *Robber and Hero*. Northfield, Minnesota, 1895.

Kansas City Daily Journal, April 4, 1882; April 5, 1882; April 6, 1882; May 6, 1882.

Kansas City Times, August 16, 1876; November 4, 1879; November 20, 1879; July 20, 1881; February 11, 1911.

Kansas City Weekly Times, April 6, 1882.

Lexington (MO) *Caucasian*, October 17, 1874.

Liberty (MO) *Tribune*, February 16, 1939.

Louisville Daily Courier, March 21, 1868.

McGrane, Martin Edward. *The James Farm*. Madison, S.D, Caleb Perkins Press, 1991.

Nashville *Banner*, March 22, 1868.

St. Joseph Western News, (week of) April 3, 1882.

St. Louis *Daily Missouri Republican*, February 16, 1866; November 3, 1866.

St. Louis *Dispatch*, June 7, 1874; June 9, 1874.

St. Louis *Globe Democrat*, November 14, 1900; February 19, 1915.

St. Louis *Missouri Republican*, April 6, 1882.

St. Louis *Post Dispatch*, November 3, 1880; June 29, 1902; February 11, 1911.

St. Louis *Republican*, November 26, 1876.

Settle, Jr., William A. *Jesse James Was His Name*. Columbia, MO, University of Missouri Press, 1966.

Steele, Phillip W., "Jesse James; Brother-in-law," *Quarterly of the National Association and Center for Outlaw and Lawman History.* Vol. X, Number 2, Fall, 1985.

Steele, Phillip W., *Jesse and Frank James: The Family History.* Gretna, LA, Pelican Publishing Company, 1994.

Yeatman, Ted P. "Allan Pinkerton and the Raid on 'Castle James,'" *True West*. Vol. 39, No. 10, October 1992. pp. 16-23.

_____. "Jesse James in Tennessee," *True West*. Vol 32, No. 4. July, 1985. pp. 1015.

_____. "The Guns of Jesse James," *Old West*. Vol. 33, No. 1. Fall, 1996. pp 20-23

A note on references: William Settle's *Jesse James Was His Name* and Phillip Steele's *Jesse and Frank James: The Family History* were invaluable for the story of the two Zereldas. Their research, both in depth and volume, is commendable.

In addition, those newspapermen and women who left behind eyewitness accounts from a century ago, are to be commended again. Despite occasional inaccuracies, the first person accounts are priceless.

Finally, the good deeds being done by the Friends of the James Farm (P.O. Box 404; Liberty, MO 64068) are also commendable. A trip to the James Farm, a tour of the house, a stroll to the stream are all necessary to have a more thorough understanding of Jesse James, the two Zereldas and their time in the history of the American West.

Allie Townsend
The Wild & Woolly West Makes A Widow

Alice Allen Townsend was preparing for supper and watching her five-year-old, Sam, Jr. It was nearing three p.m. on March 28, 1882. Allie's little house was at 605 Harrison Avenue in Leadville, the booming Colorado mining town about seventy-five miles southwest of Denver at the head of the Arkansas River valley. Leadville, just below the treeline and almost two miles above sea level, had grown quickly. Counts during this period showed 15,000, 30,000, even as many as 60,000 miners living at Leadville. The city also had a public school, 28 miles of streets, 5 miles of water mains, 3 public hospitals, 3 fire companies, 30 production mines, 10 large smelters, 6 stage lines, 3 breweries, 7 churches and a couple of hotels. There were, at different times, also 82 to 120 saloons, 118 gambling houses, 102 law firms, 140 lawyers, and 35 houses of ill repute.

In the vicinity of Harrison and Fifth, three pistol shots rang out. It was still unusual to hear gunshots on a Tuesday afternoon.

Allie Townsend wondered what it was all about.

Only minutes passed before there was a short, frenzied knock at Allie's door. The shots couldn't have involved her husband, she thought.

In 1875, Allie had married Sam Townsend, a native of Wallingford, Vermont, at Del Norte, Colorado. She was 18. At age 24, Sam was elected assessor of Rio Grande County.

He then served two terms as sheriff and two as marshal of Alamosa. They moved to Leadville in 1880.

Zach Allen of Pueblo, one of Sam's deputies, was Allie's father. Zach Allen had been killed in the line of duty. For Allie, that all came rushing back as she pulled Sam, jr. along the rutted, dusty street headed for the H.T. Dodge & Co. drugstore. Sam was there; he'd been shot.

In a hallway in the vicinity of the Union block, a rising young lawyer, Thomas C. Early, nephew of Confederate General Jubal Anderson Early of Virginia, approached Officer Samuel C. Townsend. Angry words turned into a quarrel concerning a replevia suit brought by Minnie Mordell against Carrie Adams, the proprietress of a house of ill repute. General Early claimed Townsend had overcharged him in fees "a matter of ten or fifteen cents." A struggle followed. Early managed to get at his pistol and shoot three times. One bullet "entered (Sam's) right side a little above the groin and came out on the left side of the hip." The one bullet tore through the large intestines. There was a great deal of bleeding.

By the time Mrs. Townsend arrived on the scene, her husband was laid out on a mattress at Dodge's. Lawyer Thomas C. Early, the shooter, had already been taken into custody. Early, according to witnesses, "trembled like a leaf, was pale as a sheet, and his eyes looked as if they would leap out of his head." He ran only a short distance before being apprehended. Members of the citizenry heard of the shooting and called for revenge. A crowd assembled almost immediately. Townsend was a popular and respected policeman. The sheriff's department and other police hurried Early along to the county jail for his own protection. He was locked away in solitary confinement.

As Mrs. Townsend entered Dodge's, she sensed that her husband was bad off. Dr. David H. Dougan and Dr. B. Galloway examined the wound. Judge Charles W. Tankersley, "one of the oldest and best friends of Mr. Townsend,"

had arrived. It was just a matter of minutes until Townsend
bled to death. There was nothing they could do but try to
keep him comfortable.

The drugstore door was closed and the shades were
pulled to protect the sanctity of the dying man. Mrs. Townsend and her brother-in-law, George A. Townsend, sat on
the floor beside their husband and brother. [Brother George
had moved with Sam and Allie from Del Norte, but passed
up Leadville for a 160-acre homestead at the entrance to Beaver Creek canyon across the Continental Divide in the newly
opened Eagle River valley. He was only visiting Leadville at
the time of his brother's shooting.] A lady sat at Townsend's
feet holding Sam, Jr.

Judge Tankersley looked his friend in the eye and
asked, "Sam, do you know who shot you?"

Gasping, the pain more intense now, Sam croaked,
"T.C. Early."

"What caused the trouble between you?"

"He abused me." [Some in attendance claimed later
that Townsend said something else. One faction recalled, "I
was abusing him and he gave me no cause for it." The other
claimed: "He abused me. I may have abused him and he
may have been right."]

The judge hesitated then asked, "Do you know that you
are in imminent danger?"

Through the pain on his face, Townsend replied, "I do,
you bet."

"Do you know that you are in danger and approaching
dissolution?"

Townsend nodded, "Yes."

The pain was growing more intense and Townsend
said, "Please don't bother me."

He added, to his wife, "Oh you don't know how much
misery I'm in."

Townsend's head was turning back and forth and he
said he wished he was dead. He quieted some and spoke

softly to his sobbing wife. His son, Sam, Jr., rose and knelt by his father's head. He kissed his father twice on the cheek. Townsend's eyes opened and he stared at the boy. Then, looking toward his brother, Townsend said, "Take care of the boy, George."

The dying man's eyes closed. Allie sobbed. Sam, Jr. didn't quite grasp it all. The others hung their heads in sadness.

Suddenly, Townsend's eyes were open. He raised himself on his elbows, looked at his wife, and said, "God bless you, Allie."

Three minutes later Officer Sam C. Townsend was dead. Alice Allen Townsend was a widow.

Allie's days immediately after the killing were so full of friends that she hardly had time to think or plan her future. The day after the death, Townsend lay in state at his house at No. 605 Harrison Avenue. At two o'clock that afternoon, 2,000 mourners, including the city council and police force, followed the body to the Protestant Episcopal Church of St. George. Those who could crowd into the church heard the Rev. T. J. Mackay eulogize the dead policeman. He was interred at Evergreen Cemetery.

Soon, Allie learned of the verdict of the coroner's jury. Early had done the killing. The jury recommended that Early be imprisoned in the county jail, without bail, until the grand jury met again. Sam Townsend's death certificate read, "Shot by T.C. Early, S.O.B."

Allie Townsend had nothing to keep her in Leadville. She took her son and went to live with her brother-in-law George. Just over a year later, the *Rocky Mountain News* reported on April 12, 1883, "Fifteen miles from Rock Creek, at the junction of Beaver Creek with the Eagle, G.A. Townsend, a pioneer ranchman, has a comfortable place where the casual traveler is welcome to stay while the lady of the house furnishes the best the place affords."

The following year, George and Allie went to Red Cliff and became the eighth couple to be married in Eagle County. Life went well for the newlyweds. The ranch was expanded to 400 acres. George operated a post office and stage depot. Together they had a daughter, Charlotte. But as the years passed, George's health failed. He needed a move to a warmer climate.

In 1898, George and Allie sold the ranch and moved to Florence, Colorado, near Canon City. George died there two years later. The obituary made no mention of Charlotte, but did mention an "invalid son."

Allie was left a widow again at age forty-three.

෧෨

Thomas C. Early, Attorney at Law: The details of T.C. Early's life after March 28, 1882, are sketchy. Twenty-eight at the time of the Leadville crime, he was a Virginia native and had graduated from Missouri State University. He was admitted to the bar in 1877. He had been in Leadville perhaps three years at the time of the shooting. He was a member of the law firm of Dankford & Early. He and his wife and young daughter lived on West Third Street.

Early claimed that Townsend threatened him. Early then went home for his silver-mounted pistol and returned to confront and shoot Townsend. Early claimed, "I did it in self defence."[sic]

By 1893, Early's past was behind him and he had been practicing law in Denver for ten years. The law firm of T.C. Early & J.W. Easton was located in 4467 Equitable Building. Early's partner, Easton, from Illinois, had practiced at Leadville at one time. *The Historical and Descriptive Review of Denver: Her Leading Business Houses and Enterprising Men* said of Easton and Early: "They are businesslike and painstaking lawyers, concise in argument and do a growing practice in all the State and Federal courts."

ℰↃↃℛ

Bibliography

Colorado: A Guide to the Highest State. (American Guide Series) New York, Hastings House Publishers, n.d.

Eberhart, Perry. *Guide to the Colorado Ghost Towns and Mining Camps.* Denver, Sage Books, 1959.

Griswold, Don L. and Jean Harvey Griswold. *The Carbonate Camp Called Leadville.* Denver, The University of Denver Press, 1951.

Historical and Descriptive Review of Denver: Her Leading Business Houses and Enterprising Men. Denver, Jno. Lethem, 1893.

Leadville (CO) *Daily Herald,* March 29, 30, 1882; December 4, 1900.

Martin, Cy. *Whiskey and Wild Women.* NY, Hart Publishing, Inc., 1974.

The *Rocky Mountain News* (Denver), April 12, 1883.

Simonton, June B. *Beaver Creek: The First One Hundred Years.* Beaver Creek Resort Company, 1980.

Glendolene Myrtle Kimmell
Tom Horn and the Schoolteacher

Wyoming was about as wild and woolly as the West got in the 1880s and 1890s. One such place, the Iron Mountain country, was as wild as they came. At the same time, there were those Wyoming citizens who were trying to create a civilization out of the chaos of murder and mayhem. The school district hired a schoolteacher, started a school, and began providing education. The 1900s would be a step forward for Wyoming, a step backward for lawlessness.

In Wyoming during the 1880s and 1890s, there were about forty-five ranches that made up the Wyoming Stock Growers Association. They were big spreads and owners spent a great deal of money to keep their herds safe. They saw it in their best interests to "buy" all the judges, senators and governors they could afford. Since regular lawmen didn't seem to be able to stop rustling and protect public lands, the ranchers hired stock detectives to ride over the land, protect it from homesteaders, and eliminate those who rustled cattle.

Then, nature scored a major blow. The blizzards of 1885-87 cut into the big, open range herds. Herd losses ran as high as 80 and 90 percent. Domestic cattle could not live on the open range in the middle of Northern winters with no supplemental food or shelter from the snow and cold.

It was economically disastrous for ranchers and their cattle, and equally threatening for the homesteaders. It was especially difficult for those just getting a start. Often, the cowboy who was laid off because of herd losses decided to homestead some land for himself. He might even rope a few cows and a bull to get a start, figuring that he "deserved" this start since the rancher had probably roped a few "stray" cattle himself.

To law enforcement, the theft of cattle was something they didn't want to get involved with. As a result, they became selective about *when* they'd enforce and *what* they'd enforce. This was the frontier, the lawless frontier. The ranchers saw the law as ineffective.

Politicians were securely in the pockets of the big ranchers, but that didn't seem to help much when there was a trial. When someone was tried for rustling, it seemed that the courts seldom got a conviction. Part of the reason was that there were more homesteaders and rustlers than there were big ranchers.

Ranchers panicked at these cattle losses—man-made and natural. In desperation, they hired gunmen to stop the thieving. In 1892, an army of gunmen were hired to move into the territory north of Cheyenne and exterminate about seventy suspected rustlers. The plan was a disaster since it only stirred resentment against the ranchers. Some politicians even turned down the ranchers' money. For the large cattlemen, some different tactic had to be applied.

The answer came with the skills and the methods of a tall, straight man who sometimes rode a horse named "CAP." The man's name was Horn, Tom Horn. He liked to remind his employers, "Killing men is my specialty." [Horn said it a little differently in court, "Prevention of stealing has been my business."] (Krakell, *The Saga*, p. 142.)

But if Tom Horn was a killer, he fit that role out of the necessity of the times and the frontier. Horn was hard riding, hard drinking, hard fighting. At least, that is the way that an attractive Missouri schoolteacher, Glendolene Myrtle Kimmell, viewed him.

Glendolene Myrtle Kimmell came West to teach school, but she was also looking for Tom Horn, or rather, a Westerner like Tom Horn. Horn fit the ideal image that she had of the lone cowboy fighting against all odds to tame the frontier. Tom Horn was going to be her bigger-than-life hero.

"Horn was six feet two in height, broad-shouldered and deep-chested, with an erect carriage and of great physical strength. His character has been a subject of much controversy. By his friends...he is described as a man of unfailing good nature, courteous, considerate, generous, and thoroughly honest." ("Tom Horn," *Dictionary of American Biography*.)

And Glendolene Kimmell probably saw "a straight, lean back, his brown, lean face, his sweeping mustache and his sidelong glance under a rolling sombrero." (Monaghan, p. 94.)

But how does a nice girl from Hannibal, Missouri, a schoolmarm, meet up with a hard-drinking, gunslinging character like Tom Horn? And how does the last of the gunmen mesh with the arrival of the schoolteacher?

It was the summer of 1900, and the Iron Mountain School Board advertised across the United States for a schoolteacher. Recruiters were sent into the Midwest looking for such teachers.

Glendolene Kimmell had graduated from Hannibal High School. "Several young women from Marion and Ralls County (in Missouri) went West during that period to find careers." (Hagood, July 2 & 9, 1994.)

Miss Kimmell sent a resumé and a photograph to the Iron Mountain Board. She then grew busy studying the atlas to pin down the location of the mountain of iron ore, the railroad station, and the post office in the northwest corner of Laramie County near the Chugwater. She was anxious to go West to teach.

The Iron Mountain Board met and went over her resume. She was a high school graduate. She was born in 1880 so she was about twenty. They paid more attention to her photo than anything. Some noticed her eyes and remarked that she was "slant-eyed." She had a round face and prominent eyes. Some thought she was Asiatic.

"This curiosity spread, a little later, when Miss Kimmell was employed as a teacher and arrived in the district. She chatted pleasantly in a deep voice, but her skin was sallow enough to make some observers think her part Mongolian." (Monaghan, p. 193.) There were those who claimed she'd said her birthplace was Hawaii and her ancestry German.

Glendolene Kimmell was the daughter of Elijah Lloyd Kimmell of Ohio and Frances Asenath Pierce of Hannibal, Missouri. Her father had served with the 38th Ohio Infantry in the Civil War, then taken a job with the railroad and worked for a time in an office in St. Louis.

Elijah and Frances had Glendolene Myrtle and two other children. Daisy Natalie (1870-72) was not yet two when she died. John Pierce (1865-81) died in St. Louis, and Glendolene was born in 1880.

The next year, Glendolene's father died in St. Louis. His body was transported to Hannibal and buried in Riverside Cemetery. By the mid-1880s, Glendolene and her mother were living at 321 North Fifth in Hannibal.

Glendolene attended school in Hannibal and graduated in 1899. By 1901, the Hannibal City Directory lists her mother living alone. Glendolene had moved to Wyoming. ("A List of Deaths" and *Hannibal* (MO) *City Directory: 1873-1901.*)

The Iron Mountain School Board decided to hire her. [There is no evidence that they had more than one candidate for the teaching position.] At the Miller-Nickell school, Glendolene did a satisfactory job. Very soon, people forgot any prejudices they had about her sallow complexion. Those prejudices put to rest, Glendolene got on with her teaching agenda. She had room and board with the James V. Miller family and they admired her polite manners. Someone did note, however, "Her pompadour usually parted miserably and lay flat on her head."

She liked her job, but she was disappointed with the men she met there. This was the wild and woolly West. Where were the cowboys? Where were the men of adventure, danger, and courage?

"She did not hide the fact that one reason she had left Missouri was to see the cowboys of whom she had read such romantic tales, and that in the Miller household, where she roomed and boarded, she was disappointed, since the Miller boys were only farmhands on horseback." (See Monaghan, pp. 193-94.)

She had come West for adventure and perhaps a husband, but all she found were "cattle men and cow boys" who were like the hired hands she'd encountered near her home in the Midwest. Disappointed, Kimmell had nearly decided her search was at an end when in rode Tom Horn who, in her words, embodied "the code of the frontier."

And what did Miss Kimmell see when Tom Horn stepped down from CAP? "Standing six feet two, he was built in perfect proportion to his height—broad-shouldered, deep-chested, full-hipped. Without an ounce of superfluous flesh upon him and with muscles of steel, he could perform feats of strength which were the admiration and despair of other men.

"With strong jaws, and chin, and nose, he would have been hard-featured but for the full lips which could so easily curve into a smile." (Horn, Oklahoma Press, p. 265.)

As Horn's visits continued, she learned more and more about him. He liked to spin a yarn. One writer observed, "Although he lacked much formal education, Tom was quite a linguist. He was honest and had many friends. He was not coarse in his speech except when drunk. (Launderville) And he could spice his stories with German, Spanish, and might throw in a little Apache. He told her he'd punched cattle for the Iron Mountain Cattle Company until 1898. The Spanish-American War called him away then. He said he was a mule packer for the Army. He said he'd helped organize the pack animals at St. Louis. He then helped move them to Tampa, Florida, for shipment to Cuba.

By the time "the splendid little war" ended and Tom was back in Wyoming, things were getting out of control in the fifty-square-mile region called Iron Mountain Country. Kimmell wrote, "Rustlers had grown so bold that the leading cattlemen hired Horn as a stock detective." Horn's job was to "discover offenders and prevent stealing." Kimmell admitted, "Of course, there were killings." She added, "Naturally, the rustlers blamed Horn, they hated him in proportion as they feared." (Horn, Oklahoma Press, p. 250.)

Kimmell listened to his stories of how to deal with cattle rustlers. They were exciting enough to hold the attention of any man, woman, or child. He explained how he brought these matters under control. Jay Monaghan, Horn biographer, described Horn's style. He wrote, "Tom made threats against rustlers, and ate meals in small cabins, boasting meanwhile of the murders he had committed." (Monaghan, p. 193.) He let the homesteaders know that he was bad, didn't like rustling, and didn't mind killing. Throughout central Wyoming, mothers taught their unruly children fear by threatening to call on Tom Horn to "come and get 'em."

Horn boasted of the killing he had done. He took pride in calling himself "an exterminatin' son-of-a-bitch." (Monaghan, p. 17.) As Miss Kimmel explained later, "His main weapon was his reputation as a killer." Kimmell recalled, "So it came to pass that many people believed Horn responsible for all the killings. They forgot that other stock detectives were riding, that cattlemen as well as their detectives can handle guns, and that the rustlers quarrel among themselves! The authorities could never fathom the mysterious

A 1996 photo of the Etna Methodist Church founded in 1866. It is located just a few miles from Tom Horn's boyhood home in Missouri. (Author's Collection)

killings, and the trouble went on." (Horn, Oklahoma Press, pp. 249-50.)

It was under these conditions that Tom Horn drifted into the Miller place and met Glendolene Myrtle Kimmell. Did she see herself romantically linked with Horn? Kimmell was, according to one observer, aware of "an odd little schoolma'am who attracted him mildly." (Monaghan, p. 193.)

A more modern observer points out: "It was her first acquaintanceship with a typical westerner. She admired him, liked to listen to the stories of his adventures, and they became friends. There is no reason to believe that they were lovers, as was later claimed." (Hagood, July 2 & 9, 1994.)

Still another observation comes from 1964: Leora Peters, writing in Platte County, Wyoming, noted, "They formed a mutual admiration society. It is said that Tom cared as much for Glendolene as it was in his makeup to care for any woman." ("Reminisce With Leora Peters," March 13, 1964.)

A contemporary of Horn's and Kimmell's, T. Joe Cahill said, "Horn didn't have to work very hard at being a ladies' man. They seemed to be fascinated merely by his presence. To my knowledge there was only one that he was genuinely sweet on. She was a school teacher running a grassland school north of Cheyenne. Without going into the facts of the case, I believe the schoolmarm was one of the reasons for his downfall. The other was whiskey." (Krakell, "Was Tom Horn Two Men?")

But what trail did this former scout, interpreter, Indian fighter take to James V. Miller's house and the meeting with Miss Kimmell?

Tom Horn was born to Thomas and Mary Miller Horn on November 21, 1860. [Some sources say Tom was born in 1861. However, the *U.S. Census Records*, 1880, Harrison Township, Scotland County, Missouri, collected in the summer of 1880, list Tom as age 19.] Tom's oldest brother, Charles, was born in Chautauqua, Ohio, on January 1, 1852. By the time Tom was born, the family had moved to Missouri. Tom was born in Scotland County in northeast Missouri just southeast of the county seat at Memphis. The nearest community to the Horns was Etna, a lively, friendly little frontier town in the mid-1800s. A stagecoach line connected Etna with Canton, Missouri, on the southeast and Bloomfield, Iowa, on the northwest. Canton, on the Mississippi, was their "window to the east." The stage stopped at Fairmont, Etna, Arbela, Memphis, and other settlements. For several decades, Etna was the chief trading center for northeast Missouri. (Scotland County Genealogical Society. *Scotland County, Missouri: 1841 Sesquicentennial 1991*, pp. 15-18.)

The Horns were among the first to settle in the rough clay hills of Scotland County. Thomas Horn was born in Pennsylvania. His wife, Mary A. Miller, was born in Ohio.

They settled along the banks of South Wyaconda Creek. Tom's father eventually controlled about 1,000 acres. At first, he farmed only the bottomland along the Wyaconda. The rest of his land was tall, lush grass best suited for cattle. Horn built a two-story frame house along the main road that cut through his property. Across the road, opposite the house, he built a huge barn. Mr. and Mrs. Thomas Horn then settled in for a long, God-fearing life together on the frontier.

The Horns had nine children. There were three girls, Nancy (the oldest girl), Hannah, and Maude. (Twin girls died in childbirth) Charles (the oldest), William, Austin, Martin, and Tom were the boys in the family. The children all attended the Etna Methodist Church. Since the population was mainly German, the sermons were in German and remained that way until after 1900.

Tom wrote about his parents shortly before he died. He remembered his father as a prosperous farmer and his mother as "a tall powerful woman." He also noted that his father did not spare the rod. His mother, Mary, was a "good, old-fashioned Campbellite." (Davison.)

Horn admitted, however, "Up to the time I left home I suppose I had more trouble than any man or boy in Missouri." His brother Charles had gone West and their father had bought some land near Burrton, Kansas. Tom and Charles opened Horn & Horn's Livery Stable. This was around 1880. That venture did not last long for Tom. In later years, Charles Horn remembered, "Our life in Kansas was too tame for Tom. He wasn't content to cultivate a hundred and sixty acres, drink a little whiskey, pitch horseshoes on Sunday, marry a brood woman and raise his own baseball nine." (Monaghan, p. 143.)

Horn did many frontier jobs, most of them too adventurous for an ordinary man. He claimed to have driven a stagecoach, punched cows, busted broncs, and interpreted for the Fifth U.S. Cavalry as they scoured the southwest deserts and mountains searching for Nana and Geronimo. Noted Army scout Al Sieber was his teacher between 1882 and 1885. Horn worked for Gen. Nelson A. Miles, Marion P. Maus, and others. Later, Gen. Leonard Wood revealed in his diary some of Horn's exploits. Sieber said after Horn's death, "A more faithful worker or more honorable man I never met in my life." (Krakell, *The Saga*, p. 4.)

In 1887, Tom became ill. His tonsils were causing him concern, so he returned to his Missouri home to have his tonsils removed. His mother, Mary, and sister, Nancy, took care of him, nursing him back to good health. (Monaghan, p. 43.)

On his return to the West, he took a job with the Pinkertons as an agent. Thomas "Peg Leg" Eskridge and the McCoys (Tom, Joe, and their father, "Old Dick") had robbed a train shortly before Horn went to work for the Pinkertons. Horn had heard of the opening with the Pinkertons through W.C. "Doc" Shores. Horn met Shores in 1890; Shores introduced Horn to James McParland of the Pinkertons. Along with Sheriff Shores of Gunnison County, Colorado, Horn tracked some members of the gang into New Mexico, on into Texas, back to Colorado, and into Utah. Once he ended this chore, he quit the Pinkertons. Horn wrote, "My work for them was not the kind that exactly suited my disposition; too tame for me." (Horn, Oklahoma Press, pp. 259-63.)

Horn next found work with the Swan Land & Cattle Company. He was hired by John Clay, manager of the company and president of the Wyoming Stock Growers Association. This was about 1892, and he hired on as a stock detective. In mid-October 1893, Horn was deputized by the Laramie County sheriff for the purpose of seeking out rustling suspects. A month later, the *Laramie Boomerang* had a story that included Horn: "Deputy Sheriff Horn arrived in the city this afternoon from the Sybille with five prisoners whom he had arrested [on November 12] in the Sybille country and taken across to Iron Mountain, where he boarded the train. The prisoners were Wm. Taylor, L. Bath, L. Cleve and wife and Mrs. Langhoff. All are charged with stealing cattle and killing beef."

Horn soon met and came to know and admire John C. Coble. Coble was the one-time partner with Sir Horace Plunkett in the Frontier Land & Cattle Company. Their partnership ended with the disastrous blizzards of the mid-1880s.

Coble began ranching outside of Cheyenne in the Iron Mountain, fifteen miles northwest of Laramie on the Little Laramie River. His address was Bosler, Wyoming, the town named for Frank Bosler. Coble managed the Iron Mountain Cattle Company. (Krakell, *The Saga*, p. 4.)

On Horn's visits to John Coble and to the Miller residence where Miss Kimmell got her room and board, he heard about a two-decade long feud between the Millers and Kels P. Nickell. As a matter of fact, the feud was of such importance that schoolteacher Glendolene Kimmell was made aware of it right from the beginning. She was, after all, teaching at the Miller-Nickell school. She needed to be especially aware that the boys from these two families had fought before and had threatened each other frequently. Their respective ranches lay in close proximity, affording them ample occasions to snipe at each other—name calling, cursing, threatening. [Later, Miss Kimmell learned that both Nickell and Miller disliked Coble, who had brought cattle in and pressed both of them.]

The Millers said Nickell was "an erratic, red-haired Kentuckian." As for Nickell's opinion of Miller, he saw James V. Miller as a religious fanatic. Both men had homesteaded property in the area about two decades earlier. Now it was 1901 and the most serious clash between the factions was about to happen.

There was an incident in February when Coble and Nickell had words. Nickell suddenly had a knife and was trying to stab Coble. He managed to slash Coble a couple times in the abdomen but, the cuts were not fatal. Coble had Nickell arrested; but Nickell pled self-defense and was turned loose.

Nickell and Coble's foreman had quarreled over Nickell's cattle trespassing on Iron Mountain property. Nickell's son, Willie, had threatened to run down Victor Miller with his horse. Victor's father, James V. Miller, told the Nickell boy that he'd shoot his horse if any such thing happened. And because of the feud, James V. Miller took to carrying a rifle. One day, the rifle discharged accidentally and killed one of Miller's younger sons. It would never have happened, Miller figured, if it weren't for that redheaded Kentuckian. Coble and some others were sort of hoping something might develop out of all of this that would rid the area of both Nickell and Miller. (Monaghan, p. 198.)

It was a good feud to avoid. But Tom Horn seldom walked around trouble. For that matter, Miss Kimmell was interested in being in it as well. She enjoyed studying human behavior. The ins and outs of this particular feud would bring excitement to her dull days for weeks to come. But as happens with many feuds, this one got out of hand.

Kels Nickell brought in sheep belonging to others for the purpose of raising them on public range on shares with the owners. Word spread quickly that Nickell was up to no good. In Miller's and Coble's minds, it was too much. Intolerable. It was "an unpardonable sin," wrote Glendolene Kimmell. (Horn, Oklahoma Press, p. 250.) He shouldn't have brought in the sheep. The stubborn redhead had to be dealt with. He'd gone too far.

Thursday, July 18, 1901, found fourteen-year-old Willie Nickell preparing to ride to Iron Mountain Station and meet a sheep herder from there. Actually, the herder had been at the Nickell ranch wanting work the day before, but Kels had refused to hire him.

Now, Kels had changed his mind. He wanted Willie to bring the herder back. And since it was a cold, damp, overcast day, Kels told his oldest son to wear his father's hat and rain slicker. The boy hadn't been feeling well. He didn't want him getting sick from the damp.

Willie grabbed a handful of mane and pulled himself into the saddle. He turned the horse and rode toward a wire gate less than a mile from the Nickell's house.

The boy left his mother, Mary Nickell, between 6:30 and 6:50 a.m. She heard two shots about 20 minutes later, but thought nothing of it. One and a half miles east of the Nickell ranch house, Kels Nickell and two other men were busy surveying. There would be a delay in finding the fourteen-year-old who had dressed himself in some of his father's old clothes that overcast morning when the light was not good for shooting.

When Willie did not show up for the evening meal, there was some concern. When the boy did not show up for breakfast, the parents, especially Mary, became alarmed. They waited for the children to leave the table, then discussed what to do. If Willie wasn't back by noon, they'd start a search.

In the meantime, there was the normal routine to follow. Another son, Fred, was sent to take the cows to pasture. He rode toward the wire gate less than a mile from the Nickell's house. Tragically young Fred found his brother Willie's body.

In a state of panic, Fred spun his horse and kicked the animal toward the ranch house. He sobbed as he lashed at the horse.

Hearing the approaching hooves, Kels Nickell and those helping with the surveying charged out the back door. "Will has been murdered!" Fred screamed.

The Laramie County sheriff and Coroner Thomas Murray were on the scene in a few hours. Willie was hit twice on the left side, once in the chest and once in the abdomen. The second shot entered in the back. They carefully went over the crime scene and found nothing. They found no clues and made no arrests. It was a baffling crime. (Krakell, *The Saga*, p. 17.)

On July 22, there was an inquest. It seemed to some that Miller's son, Victor, probably killed Willie as an outgrowth of past fights. Glendole Kimmell observed, "The evidence was not strong enough to warrant an arrest, and it looked as though this tragedy would also remain unsolved." (Horn, Oklahoma Press, pp. 250.)

For Kels Nickell, it was inconceivable that someone could have shot his unarmed, fourteen-year-old son in the back. But he was determined to stay on his homestead. He made the statement, "The worst has passed, why leave now?"

But if the worst was past, there was still some bad to come. On August 4, Kels went out to drive some calves off an alfalfa patch. Just over a quarter of a mile from the house, all hell broke loose. Bullets were flying around him and he began a zigzag run for the house. A firey pain ripped through him as he was hit in the left arm, in the left hip, and in the right arm. He was taken to Cheyenne for treatment. He complained that it was the Millers who had tried to kill him. Kels said, "Tom Horn will get the blame for this, but he never done it." He added, "Victor Miller is the guilty man." (Monaghan, p. 197.)

As Kels Nickell lay in a Cheyenne hospital, four masked men attacked his herd of sheep. Out of a herd of 1,000, they killed about 75. The sheep herder, an Italian immigrant, was threatened and fled the area. He began walking and didn't stop until he covered the forty miles to Cheyenne.

No question, this feud had gotten out of hand. People in southeastern Wyoming were up in arms. It had been nearly ten years since the Johnson County War. The lawless hangings, the killings from ambush, were events left behind in the nineteenth century. This new century, the twentieth, had to be better.

A determined posse left Cheyenne to round up the accused Millers. A crowd of 200 waited at the depot in Cheyenne when James V. Miller and his sons, Victor and August, were brought in. No shots were fired. There was no resistance.

In the meantime, Laramie County Sheriff Shafer became ill. He contacted Deputy U.S. Marshal Joe LeFors to come in on the case. LeFors was familiar with Wyoming cattle trouble. Born in Paris (Lamar County), Texas, during 1865, he was just twenty when he took a job with the Murphy Cattle Company driving cattle to Montana. Ten years later, he had a job as a livestock inspector and moved to Newcastle in northeastern Wyoming. At the time of the Willie Nickell shooting, he was working on a counterfeit case in Aladdin, in Crook County, Wyoming. (Brown, pp. 6-9.)

LeFors agreed to enter the case, but only if he could work undercover. (Krakell, *The Saga*, pp. 17-21.) Laramie County and the State of Wyoming had put up rewards of $500 each. Some have suggested that the $1,000 reward is what attracted Marshal LeFors. (Monaghan, p. 199.)

At a second session of the coroner's inquest, the brothers and sisters of Willie Nickell testified that they had seen the shooters ride away. They all said the two riflemen rode off toward the Miller ranch. One rode a bay. The other was on a gray.

Nickell had seen enough. He was the oldest homesteader south of Iron Mountain, but while still in his hospital bed, he sent word to his wife to move with the children to Cheyenne. Put the place up for sale, he ordered. Nickell had been there in the Iron Mountain District nearly twenty years, but he knew when he was licked. [By October 1902, Kels Nickell was working as a night watchman for the Union Pacific Railroad in Cheyenne. Another source (Krakell, *The Saga*, p.4) says Nickell opened a steam laundry in Cheyenne.]

There were those who *thought* Tom Horn might be involved. A few were brave enough to *say* they thought Horn was involved, and the Millers talked about him taking part. August and Victor Miller, James V. Miller's sons, told Kimmell, "It's all right to let suspicion fall on Tom Horn! He doesn't care and it might help us." (Horn, Oklahoma Press, p. 251.)

Glendolene Kimmell, still taking room and board in the Miller house, testified. She'd seen Victor Miller about 8:30 in the moring. James V. Miller was there too, but she only heard him moving about, singing a bit.

Had she known about the feud? She testified: "When the school was offered to me the trouble between the two families was fully explained to me."

And what had she observed about this feud? What had she concluded about Nickell and Miller? She answered, "Two men were thrown together whose natures were respectively such that they could not get along." (Carlson, *Tom Horn: "Killing...,"* p. 118.)

Because of confusion over whether or not Victor Miller was in the house, all of Miss Kimmell's testimony was thrown out. Her testimony neither accused nor acquitted Horn.

By early September, Tom Horn had other things on his mind. He and some friends from Albany County came to Cheyenne and won first honors in Frontier Days festivities. (*Laramie Boomerang*, September 1, 1901.)

Horn next took a load of horses to Denver and got his jaw broken in a brawl. His jaw was healed enough by December to return to some of the final days of the inquest from the Kels Nickell shooting. He was called to testify and eliminated himself as a suspect.

With Marshal LeFors on the case, he began stirring up the countryside. He rode out to Miller's ranch and questioned Miss Kimmell. There was something suspicious about LeFors in Kimmell's eyes. He was up to something. Could he be plotting against Horn?

Kimmell wrote Tom a letter expressing these views. Over the next weeks, the letter made the rounds, going through several post offices, tracking the elusive Horn. It finally returned from Denver to Cheyenne. There Horn read the letter.

One biographer of Horn noted that Tom was busy spending his money on "the big blond." He added, "The big blonde promised more entertainment." He claimed that Horn remembered Glendolene Kimmell "with the casualness of a man recalling a collie pup who had once fawned upon him."

Horn had planned to go to Coble's for the fall. But this letter, according to Historian Jay Monaghan, worried Horn. Kimmell was surely waiting for him to return to Iron Mountain. He remained in Cheyenne.

Was he careless with Miss Kimmel's affections? An observation made by Carlson and others was that "Tom never developed any kind of deep, long-term personal relationships with women or even men, for that matter. The friendships he did have were of a professional nature, related to his work." [Monaghan speculated, "She bored him, and boredom was horrible to a killer."] (Monaghan, p. 198-99.)

"Insofar as women were concerned," Carlson noted, "Horn consequently never learned to respect the perspicacity of their intuition." A case in point is the warning by Kimmell that U.S. Deputy Marshal LeFors was up to something. And Horn had better watch out. (Carlson, *Tom Horn: "Killing…"*, p. 120.)

As to the letter about LeFors trying to slip him up, there was nothing to that, he figured. He knew LeFors. Besides, he could prove that he was on a train between Laramie and Cheyenne on the day of the killing.

In the meantime, LeFors quietly went about the business of police work. He interviewed anyone who might have the slightest information about the shootings.

It was a different southeastern Wyoming now. The sheep were gone. Rustlers had been intimidated. Somebody—Horn or someone else—had shot or would shoot anyone insane enough to try rustling. It was fall, and Tom Horn's services were no longer needed.

And then it was late December, and Deputy U.S. Marshal Joe LaFors put the word out that Horn's services were needed in Montana. A man from Montana had written LeFors. The December 28, 1901, letter to LeFors talked of a gang on Big Moon River. W.D. Smith of Miles City, the author of the letter, suggested that someone was needed to go underground for a while. Coble volunteered Horn's services, but Horn would have the last say. If Horn wanted it, LaFors, who had met Horn at Frontier Days in Cheyenne, would help Horn get the job. (Krakell, *The Saga*, p. 199.) A letter for Horn came to John C. Coble's address. It was agreeable with Horn. Someone was in Cheyenne from Montana and wanted to meet Horn. On January 7, 1902, Horn wrote that he'd be in Cheyenne to meet the agent.

Horn had good reasons to move on. He may have considered the shootings, Miss Kimmell, and civilization moving in. In short, he may have been bored. Montana sounded good. They would appreciate his help there.

Since Horn was leaving Wyoming for Montana, his friends threw a going-away party. It was nothing fancy. Just good friends getting together. Horn was some relieved, being able to leave behind his Wyoming problems. There was a party in Laramie and one in Cheyenne.

Marshal LeFors was looking for Horn. Horn had made an appointment with LeFors, but Horn missed the meeting. He was never hard to find. He had nothing to fear from LeFors. Horn was on his way to Montana. He'd be gone soon, besides, LeFors was a friend.

LeFors found Horn and they stepped down the street to LeFors' office where one of the most famous "confessions" in Wyoming—or even Western—history was made. The date was January 12, 1902, a Sunday. What was said? Kimmell insists, "There are two accounts—one is Horn's and the other Joe LeFors and his confederates." (Horn, p. 253.)

One version has Horn still half drunk when he and LeFors walked to the marshal's office. There they had more drinks, then more talk, then more drinks, and more talk. Tom talked a lot. He even said things that he claimed later he hadn't said.

In the meantime, in an adjoining room with part of the bottom of the door cut away, Charles J. Ohnhaus, district court stenographer, took down the conversation while lying on the floor and listening under the door. With Ohnhaus was Deputy Sheriff Leslie Snow. Snow was acting as a witness.

And there were more drinks and more talk.

Tom Horn hardly looked the role of the killer that he was. But Old West days were fading fast when he got all spruced up for this photograph. (Author's collection)

Was Horn drunk? LeFors claimed Horn arrived on Sunday morning, January the 12th. LeFors met him at the Union Pacific depot. LeFors said, "He was not drunk." (Krakell, *The Saga*, pp. 46-50.) Cheyenne Chief of Police D.A. "Sandy" McNeal saw Horn the morning he came in on the train. McNeal passed him on the stairs leading to the Marshal's office. To McNeal, Horn was not drunk, but "noisy and talkative." And others came forward and testified that Horn looked sober. There were still others, however, who testified that he was either drunk, or drinking. (Krakell, *The Saga*, pp. 89-90.) Horn testified, "I had not been to bed the night before; I had been up visiting, drinking, having a good time." (Krakell, *The Saga*, p. 175.)

When the drinking and the talking in LeFors office stopped, and Ohnhaus was done taking notes from the room next door, it was necessary to get his notes transcribed. By Monday morning, LeFors was sure he had what he wanted.

On January 13, 1902, Horn sat in a leather chair in the lobby of the InterOcean Hotel talking to a Union Pacific special agent, when in walked his friend, Laramie County Sheriff Edwin Smalley. Deputy R.A. Proctor was along, as was Cheyenne Chief of Police Sandy McNeal.

Smalley walked up to Horn and told him he had a warrant for his arrest. The charge was for the July 18, 1901, murder of 14 year-old Willie Nickell. Horn offered no resistance. (Brown) (Krakell, *The Saga*, p. 54.)

Horn was held without bail. The preliminary hearing on January 24 was before Justice of the Peace Joe Reed. Stenographer Charles Ohnhaus was there. So were Deputy Snow and Marshal LeFors. They explained how they rigged the door and listened to the confession. They said that Horn admitted killing the boy, Willie Nickell, and shooting at Kels Nickell. They claimed Horn threw in a couple more unsolved murders. LeFors testified that Horn was stone-cold sober at the confession. The trial was called for May 1902, but postponed to October.

The attorneys for Horn were headed up by Judge John W. Lacey, the general attorney for the Union Pacific Railroad. Lacey, an Indiana native, had an understanding of the differences between the cattle barons and the small ranchers. Others assisting were T.E. Burke, T. Blake Kennedy, Edward T. Clark, and R.N. Watson.

Walter Riggs Stoll was the prosecutor. He graduated forty-sixth in a class of fifty-two with the U.S.M.A. West Point class of 1881. He served in the Frontier Army until he resigned in 1885. An ambitious Democrat, he was in his third term as district attorney. If he could find Horn guilty, surely he'd be swept back into office. (Monaghan, p. 221.)

Judge Richard H. Scott was presiding. He had been a member of the Wyoming bar for sixteen years. Kimmell hoped that Scott would take care of Horn as he did the cattle barons.

There were more legalities to be taken care of. There was an argument for a November trial, but that was disallowed. October 7, 1901, was set as the date of trial. There were more delays and the trial finally got underway on October 13, 1902.

The 10 o'clock train from Denver whistled its arrival right on time in Cheyenne that morning. Glendolene Myrtle Kimmell stepped onto the platform. She looked small and lonely for a few moments amid the clatter of loading and unloading. The big steam locomotive hissed and then rolled out of the depot.

After the noisy engine pulled out of town, the platform was still busy with swarming people and luggage handlers getting their gear together. Some turned and entered the depot. Kimmell, a red tam pinned in place on a knot of hair at the top of her head, talked to a gang of reporters. They were nipping and snatching at every word she uttered. She had come to Cheyenne with one purpose. She was there to help one of the most fascinating men she'd ever known—Tom Horn.

Since January 1902, Horn had been locked away in a cell in the Laramie County jail. Glendolene Kimmell had plans to save the frontiersman-scout-cowboy-gunfighter. She reminded reporters of Horn's military record in the Spanish-American War. He shouldn't be treated like a common criminal. Finally, she headed for the courthouse at the corner of 19th and Carey. ("Tom Horn: Legends of the West," p. 34.)

A huge crowd pressed into the courthouse, but there were not enough seats for everyone. There wasn't even room for local residents, let alone visitors from out of town. Hotels were full, and some Cheyenne residents were taking in boarders.

Besides Miss Kimmell, John Coble was there. Victor Miller and Kels Nickell had seats. And finally, a palefaced Tom Horn was brought in wearing a dark suit. Deputy Leslie Snow accompanied him. The two didn't like each other, but Horn was calm and walked easy. Some thought he looked confident and unlikely to be found guilty.

A jury was selected. Miss Kimmell looked over the jury, "the majority of whom were cattle rustlers." At least that was the way she viewed them. She feared that they'd find the stock detective, Tom Horn, guilty of murder. She also remembered the words of "a prominent ranchman," "Show me a cattleman who's against Tom Horn, I'll show you a rustler." [A list of names of the jurors and their occupations can be found in the October 25, 1903, *Cheyenne Daily Leader*. Six were "ranchmen," one was a "cowboy," two were ranch "foremen," and there was a butcher, porter, and blacksmith.]

It became obvious to Miss Kimmell and some others that the "confession" was all that the prosecution had. LeFors read the confession aloud to those assembled in the courtroom. Horn said those sentences and phrases were not how he talked. Miss Kimmell noted, "The so-called confession was not in the language of Horn, filled as it was with profanity and vulgarity, and it is a well known fact that Horn, drunk or sober, was never vulgar and seldom profane." (Horn, Oklahoma Press, pp. 254-57.)

It was important to the jury whether or not Horn was drunk at the time of the confession. And was the confession true? And legal? Attorney Burke made the opening speech for defense. He pointed out, "A confession must be seriously, willingly and purposely made!" Lacey followed, agreeing that Horn was not drunk at the confession, but had been drinking all night and must have been under the influence of alcohol. (Krakell, *The Saga*, p. 203.)

Horn took the stand and testified that he was many miles from Nickell's ranch when he learned of the killing. Otto Plaga testified that he saw Horn on Sybille Creek. Plaga said Horn was telling the truth and couldn't have killed Willie Nickell. (Monaghan, p. 221.)

Horn testified, "I never had anything to do with the killing of Willie Nickell; I never had any cause to kill him. And I never killed him." (Krakell, *The Saga*, p. 115.)

In just a few days, the trial was over. The prosecutor had summed up in five hours. He talked about Tom's bad reputation. He said Horn worked as a detective for Coble, and Coble was an enemy of Kels Nickell. He reminded the jury that Horn was at Millers the day before Willie's death. He determined that Willie was killed by a smokeless .30-30. For good measure, he threw in testimony from two characters from Denver who claimed to have heard Tom's admission of guilt at Denver's Scandinavian Saloon.

Horn's attorney Lacey said, "I ask you to consider every single fact. Certainly not one of the state's points has been proved beyond a reasonable doubt. It will be to you a pleasant duty to give to life and liberty the protection allowed by law. I thank you, gentlemen." (Monaghan, p. 225.)

The jury was locked in a room at 11 a.m. on October 23. A juror became ill and there was fear of a mistrial. The trial had cost the county $30,000. They could never try Horn again. Laramie County could never afford it. And how would it reflect on county officials? And the governor's run for another term?

The next day, October 24, 1902, after five hours of deliberation, the verdict came in. *The Cheyenne Daily Leader*, October 25, 1902, screamed the verdict:

HORN GUILTY!!!

Jury Brought In A Verdict Yesterday
Afternoon At Just 4:37 o'clock

Horn was sentenced to be hanged between 10 a.m. and 3 p.m. on January 9, 1903. Horn remained calm through all his courtroom appearances. Was he really guilty? Why didn't he speak up?

Was the trial fair? The verdict and the story of Tom Horn are still debated. One view comes from a column in

Glendolene Myrtle Kimmell

This Hannibal, Missouri, schoolteacher did all in her power to save the famous Tom Horn from the gallows. (Photo courtesy of American Heritage Center, University of Wyoming)

Platte County, Wyoming. Leora Peters concluded ("Reminisce With Leora Peters," March 13, 1964.), "The trial was a farce. Experts testified that Willie was shot with a larger caliber rifle than Tom's and twenty-two-year-old cowboy, Otto Plaga, swore that he had seen Tom riding along Sybille Creek, twenty-five miles from the Nickell ranch at the time of the murder."

Appeals were quickly made. Defense attorneys cited seventy-nine errors. Judge Scott denied the appeal because Prosecutor Stoll was ill. By November 8, Horn's attorney, Burke, filed an appeal and cited twenty-three reasons for a new trial.

Not much came of it all. Wyoming's Supreme Court Chief Justice made the following statement: "The Supreme Court did not determine Tom Horn's guilt or innocence; they simply passed upon whether or not there had been evidence enough before the jury upon which a verdict could be passed." He added, "I have not yet made up my mind whether he is guilty or innocent. (Horn, Oklahoma Press, p. 257.)

And on and on it went, both sides sparring for an opening. There was a stay of execution and a ruling by the Wyoming Supreme Court. The Supreme Court finally refused the appeal.

Horn decided to try an appeal to human nature. He wrote to Charles Ohnhaus, the court stenographer who heard the "drunken confession." Horn complained about statements in the confession that he'd not made, or statements that were altered before being submitted to the courts. Horn appealed to Ohnhaus' honesty: "Do you want to go through life knowing, as you do, that your perjured testimony took my life?" He added, "I am appealing to you for the *truth* only."

On October 12, Horn wrote his friend Coble and told him about the appeal to Ohnhaus. Horn said he had received no answer. He wondered if Coble might try to help in the matter of Ohnhaus. He added, "You know that there is no time to spare if this thing is to be brought around." (Horn, Oklahoma Press, pp. 274-78.)

Among the citizens of Wyoming and Cheyenne, there was consternation over whether or not Horn might escape. There had been two attempts already. One escape plot called for a friend to bring off the escape by blowing up a part of the jail. A youngster named Herr, "a short-term jail inmate," was to carry the message. When the saddle thief was released, he got cold feet and disclosed the plot to the *Wyoming Tribune*. In return, the young man known as Herr received free transportation out of Wyoming. The newspaper ran the story on January 21, 1903.

On August 10, Sunday a.m., 1903, there was another attempt. This called for Horn and a fellow inmate, Jim McCloud, to overpower the Jailer Proctor. All went well, but Horn and McCloud only ran a short distance before being recaptured. This attempt served to shake up Cheyenne's citizenry. There were calls for blood, and Les Snow, the deputy, tried to bash in Horn's head with a rifle butt. He failed when a Cheyenne policeman shielded Horn and suffered a broken arm on behalf of Horn's head.

After the Wyoming governor received threatening mail, he called out Company E and Troop A of the Wyoming National Guard. That was just hours before the scheduled hanging. The guard also set up a military cordon around the jail. In order to get through this protection, an official pass was needed. A shiny Gatling gun was set up and manned by Sgt. Mahon from Fort D.A. Russell. (Krakell, *The Saga*, p. 216.)

In the meantime, teacher Glendolene Kimmell was trying to save Tom Horn from the gallows. She claimed to have overheard some men talking of killing the Nickell's boy. When this information became public, she fled Wyoming. At least one observer thinks Kimmell fled because she was afraid for her life. Still, when she heard that Horn was about to be hanged, she returned to try and help him.

But Miss Kimmell's efforts backfired. Despite her efforts to help Horn, she angered Cheyenne officials instead. One official that she angered was Wyoming Gov. Fenimore Chatterton. Kimmell presented Gov. Chatterton with an affidavit saying that James V. Miller's son Victor killed Willie Nickell. She said she did not speak up earlier because she'd been assured by Horn's lawyers that he'd be acquitted. Gov. Chatterton said this wasn't so. Miss Kimmell, he let it be known, "was not telling the truth but seeking to shield Horn."

What, exactly did Kimmell know? She knew what she'd heard at the Miller ranch. James V. Miller admitted to her that his son, Victor, had confessed to killing Willie Nickell. Then on October 10, 1901, Victor Miller confessed to Kimmell that he was the killer. Kimmell wrote later, "I agreed to say nothing provided they would make no attempt to sidetrack the crime on Horn." She concluded, rather naively, "I thought that by my continued silence I could save Victor Miller, and yet not jeopardize Horn." (Horn, Oklahoma Press, p. 256.)

After Horn was found guilty, Kimmel was ready to step forward and tell all. But the lawyers advised against this. They said that these things could not be brought forward at that time due to technicalities. When the case finally went to the governor on appeal, that would be the time to tell the rest of her story. At least, that is what Kimmell claimed that she was told.

With everything in place, she delivered the affidavit to Gov. Fenimore Chatterton. His decision dripped with politics. According to Kimmell, "a prominent lady" said, "The governor of Wyoming does not believe in capital punishment personally, but he does politically." (Horn, Oklahoma Press, p. 263.)

There were other affidavits. One attested to Victor Miller threatening Willie Nickell's life at a July 4, 1901, dance. (Krakell, *The Saga*, p. 226.) Another who testified about a Denver conversation where Horn supposedly admitted killing Nickell, wrote a letter to Attorney Lacey, "I don't think we ought to let this matter drop now and let Horn be hung without our doing the square thing." The man, Frank Mullock, felt that he had been duped into testifying to a conversation with a man posing as Tom Horn.

The national press got caught up in the Horn-Kimmell story now. From the *The Cincinnati Enquirer*, Sunday, Nov. 1, 1903:

SWEETHEART
Of Tom Horn, Condemned Murderer, Tells Wyoming's Governor That Another Committed the Crime.

SPECIAL DISPATCH TO THE ENQUIRER

Cheyenne, Wyo., October 31. This afternoon an attorney for Tom Horn appeared before Governor (Fenimore) Chatterton to make an effort in behalf of the condemned murderer of Willie Nickell. The most sensational affidavit was that of Gwendoline Myrtle Kimmell, the little schoolteacher whom Tom Horn, claimed as his sweetheart, and who disappeared before the trial of Horn came up and could not be found. The affidavit is sworn to in Jackson County, Missouri, to which place the schoolteacher went. Miss Kimmell arrived in Cheyenne last night and appeared with the attorney before Governor Chatterton this afternoon.

She affirms that on three different occasions she overheard Victor Miller and his father make statements incriminating Victor in the killing of Willie Nickell. That on one of these occasions she was in her room after supper without the knowledge of the two. Victor came in and seemed excited. His father said: "Don't get so 'tarnal excited. No one suspects you of this and it will blow over. They think Tom Horn did it."

The local press, however, was not always so friendly. Kimmell felt the stories they ran were out to hang Horn. She wrote, "They printed great masses of damaging lies, and would not admit the smallest favorable point." (Horn, Louthan Book Company, p. 284.)

On November 3, 1903, Prosecutor Stoll retaliated against the Kimmell affidavit by calling her a liar. He filed a complaint of perjury against her. A warrant was issued for Kimmell's arrest. At 2 p.m. Kimmell appeared before a Cheyenne justice of the peace. T. T. Clark and John Coble put up bail of $2,000. A hearing before the governor was held at 2 p.m. on November 5.

On November 4, a stack of affidavits was presented to the governor. On the same day, the Supreme Court ruled that the execution should be carried out between 9 a.m. and 3 p.m. on November 20.

On November 10, shortly before noon, Judge Richard Scott issued a bench warrant for the arrest of Miss Kimmell. Stoll filed a charge of perjury. Stoll added that he would file

Tom Horn was whiling away the hours, days, and weeks waiting for his appointment with the gallows. Here he braids a hackamore. (Author's collection)

charges against any perjurer. [Apparently Stoll had no thoughts about nominating LeFors, Ohnhaus, or Snow for that distinction.] Miss Kimmell's affidavit charged Victor Miller with the murder of Willie Nickell. She was held on an apparent second bond of $2,000.

On November 14, Gov. Chatterton ruled that the hanging must go on as planned. He refused to go against the findings of the lower and higher courts. And he rejected the information in the affidavits, saying the evidence should have been introduced at the trial. But he pointed out that none of the affidavits would have been permissible in a court of law. Therefore, a new trial would have added nothing new and Horn would have been guilty a second time. [And the county would have been out another $30,000, or so.] He added that he did not think that the Kimmell affidavit was true. "I do not believe that the law and justice would be served by the interposition of executive clemency." (Krakell, *The Saga*, pp. 251-52.)

Two days before the hanging, Cheyenne was a busy place. It started with a cold, clear morning. There was a slight breeze that carried away smoke from the chimneys in town. Trains were prowling around in the rail yards, huffing and hissing. The court docket set the Kimmell perjury case for the next week.

The next day, Gov. Chatterton had his last word on the Horn hanging. He said, "You may state that no respite will be granted Horn. He will hang tomorrow." (Monaghan, p. 254.)

In her hotel room, Glendolene Kimmell was grieved by it all. Why was Tom Horn being hanged? Kimmell asked herself. "Because of a drunken talk," she admitted. Horn had admitted to her that he and LeFors were boasting and trading lies in the time-honored fashion of the American West. It was the stuff that had fed stories of every tall tale from Paul Bunyan, to John Henry, to Pecos Bill.

Kimmell wrote, "He was truthful in the ordinary affairs of life, but if the spinning of a yarn would give pleasure, he was not one to let facts stand in the way." (Horn, Oklahoma Press, pp. 261-62.)

Another point that bothered Kimmell and made her think the confession was a hoax had to do with both she and Coble. Horn seemed to be turning against them, when they may have been the best friends he had at that time. Horn had said some pretty harsh things about them and for no reason.

In the so-called confession, Horn was supposed to have said of Miss Kimmell, "I don't put much stock in the school-marm. She is quarter Jap, half Samoan, and the rest just German." (Monaghan, p. 198.) Horn even apologized for what had been said about Coble. Just minutes before the hanging, Horn wrote Coble, "Your name was not mentioned in the marshal's office." (Horn, Louthan Book Company, p. 284.)

In his last letter, written just minutes before he was hanged, Horn stood by his earlier statements: "Everything that was sworn to by those fellows was a lie, made up before I came to Cheyenne." All three—LeFors, Snow and Ohnhaus—lied. Those were Tom Horn's last words on the matter. (Horn, Oklahoma Press, p. 266.)

Tom had had a lot of time to wile away. He spent twenty-two months in jail. He braided hair ropes and hackamores. He'd learned how to do that in the Southwest. He also wrote an autobiography onto 500 large-sized letter pages. Of course, it only went to 1894, as he put it, "since which time everybody else has been more familiar with my life and business than I have been myself."

Horn often wrote to members of his family, some still in Missouri, others not. His oldest sister, Nancy, wrote from Missouri in November. Another sister wrote from Elgin, British Columbia. She had named her little daughter Thomasene after Tom. Charles and Martin Horn were in town for the hanging. Tom's mother was still alive, and he mailed her two letters on the day he was hanged.

A priest, Father John Kennedy, came to visit. An Episcopal minister, Rev. John Watson, also visited. There were others, too. Some figured their stock in trade might go up some if they could save this sinner. Horn also spent some time reading the Gospel of St. John. Rev. Watson told the guards and deputies that Horn was preparing to die. "He knows there is no help for him but in God. He is ready," Watson added. (Monaghan, p. 257.)

The gallows, designed by Cheyenne architect James P. Julian, was built next to Horn's cell. Officials threw up a canvas tarp to visually separate Horn and the platform, but the constant hammering got on his nerves. He finally called to Sheriff Smalley, "Take that damned tarp down, Eddie. They's nobody more interested in seein' this than me."

On hanging day, Horn kept control. In his cell and while straightening his bunk, he said, "Can't let this thing get me down; all of us gotta go sometime."

John Coble was back on November 20. Choking back tears, Coble said, "Tom, fate's against you. You must die."

Smiling, Horn said, "You did all you could for me. I'll die all right, John."

Coble was in tears as Horn said, "Keep your nerve, John, for I'll keep mine. You know Tom Horn."

It was crowded in front of the jail when Coble came out. He told those around him, "I did all I could to save the law from hanging an innocent man. I now give up! I can do no more. Sometime the truth may be known...." (Krakell, *The Saga*, pp. 258-59.)

Inside, officials continued to test the water-operated gallows. The victim would hang himself by stepping onto a platform. When the proper amount of water trickled out of a bucket, a weight slipped off a cross arm and the trap door was sprung. A half-hour before the execution, Horn listened to the mechanism as the water, gurgled then poured, and finally triggered the latch. Horn listened to the weight snap at the end of the rope.

Would his neck break? Would death be quick and silent? Did they have everything measured right, or would Horn's handsome head pop loose from the spinal column? Such grisly imperfections were not uncommon in a land where a call for swift justice overlooked caution.

It was strangely quiet in the cell block while the equipment was tested. Then someone asked, "Ready, Tom?"

Horn stood, laid his cigar aside, walked out the cell door and about six feet to a position beside the trap. The witnesses had already filed in.

Horn looked them over, then smiled at Sheriff Ed Smalley and said, "Ed, that's the sickest looking lot of damned sheriffs I ever saw."

His friends, Big Charlie and Little Frank Irwin, had asked to sing a hymn. Tom requested a Baptist song, "Life's Railway to Heaven."

Keep your hand upon the throttle,
And your eye upon the rail.
Put your trust in Jesus;
Never falter, never fail.

There were few dry eyes in the onlookers when the Irwins finished. Horn, however, stayed firm. ("This Is Anniversary," November 30, 1933.)

With the hymn ended, Charlie Irwin called out, "Be game."

"You bet I will," Tom nodded.

Deputy Sheriff Richard A. Proctor adjusted the black hood. County Clerk T. Joseph Cahill helped Horn toward the trap door. Horn asked, "Ain't losin' your nerve, are you, Joe?" Horn smiled. Cahill said later, "It was a shaking experience. He thanked me."

Horn liked young Mr. Cahill. At one point, Horn said, "Joe, they tell me you're married now. I hope you're doing well. Treat her right." (Donoho, p. 19.)

Proctor, with Tom's help, dropped the hood over Horn's head. And then Horn was on the trap door.

It took a half of a minute for the running water to trip the trap door. One source said that the 13-wrap noose slammed against Horn's head, knocking him unconscious. It did not break his neck. He did not die instantly. A physician could find no pulse after 17 minutes. (Krakel, *The Saga*, pp. 263-64.) It was 11:08 a.m.

On the day of the hanging, Glendolene Kimmell was still being held for perjury and was under house arrest in a hotel room overlooking the courthouse where Tom's cell and gallows were housed. [Officials were still saying that she had perjured herself in trying to save Horn, her lover.]

"Glendolene had sent a frantic request to Hannibal for messages as to her respectability and the stability of her family. About a dozen prominent men sent protests to the Wyoming governor and vouched for her character." (Hagood, July 2 & 9, 1994.)

But it was all too late. She summed up what had happened to her friend Tom. "Riding hard, drinking hard, fighting hard, so passed his days, until he was crushed between the grindstone of two civilizations." (Horn, Oklahoma Press, p. 266.)

The day after Tom Horn strangled to death at the end of the hangman's noose, Glendolene Myrtle Kimmell was released from arrest. All charges were dropped. The arrest had been an error, she was told.

Tired and out of money, Kimmell caught the Denver train. She took a job at the Equitable Building and began work on a manuscript that she titled "The True Life of Tom Horn." It was never published.

By 1907, Glendolene was back home living with her mother in Hannibal. She remained there, unmarried. In

1911, she was working as a stenographer. But in 1913, Glendolene and her mother departed for Atascadero, California, in a real estate venture. The community was founded as "a real estate venture and a 'model' colony. Her mother, Frances, built a new home and Glendolene joined her. After her mother died in 1930, Glendolene "returned (to Hannibal) to bury her mother at Riverside." J. Hurley Hagood and his wife Roberta, Hannibal historians, add, "As far as we know, that was her last return to Hannibal." (Hagood, July 2 & 9, 1994.)

Glendolene's whereabouts from 1930 is not known. When and where did she die? Did she marry? Did she continue to reside in California? Tom Horn's brother, Charles had left Kansas and moved to Boulder, Colorado, in 1890. He was engaged in the teamster business and was married to Elizabeth Blattner. Charles saw to it that Tom's body was properly taken care of.

Tom was transported to Gleason and Company's Undertaking Parlors mortuary. From there, he was returned to Boulder with his brother Charles. (Horan, *The Gunfighters*, p. 254.)

Buchheit Undertaking conducted the services in Boulder. The Boulder (CO) *Daily Camera* of November 23, 1903, said, "The funeral of the late Tom Horn occurred from the Buchheit undertaking rooms Sunday afternoon and was largely attended from the outside. A respectful crowd heeded the admonition 'Funeral Private' posted on the door.... A crowd followed the remains to the grave in Boulder cemetery."

Mary Horn, Tom's mother, was at the services. Tom was buried in Pioneer Cemetery about 100 yards west of the corner of 9th Street and College Avenue in Boulder.

Charles wrote Tom's friend, John Coble:

"Kind Friend:

"We buried Tom with all due respect that relatives and friends could show. We had the largest funeral that was ever in this town. Everybody showed due courtesy to the hearse as it went seven blocks. They stood on the street with their hats off as we passed along. When we arrived at the cemetery there was hardly standing room. There must have been anyhow 2,500 people at the funeral." (Horn, Louthan Book Company, p.244.)

Continuing, Charles said he'd received Horn's belongings from "Sheriff Smalley"; he also put a guard on the grave. Attorney T.E. Burke of Cheyenne had suggested this.

Charles Horn died in 1932. His wife died in 1940. Another of Tom's sisters, Mrs. E.W. Prosser, resided in Briggsdale, Colorado, northeast of Denver. (Krakell, *The Saga*, p. 255.)

Afterword

"I am convinced, and I reassert it to be true, that Tom Horn was guiltless of the crime for which he died."
John C. Coble, Manager
Iron Mountain Cattle Company

The following is the obituary for Tom Horn that appeared in the *Memphis* (MO) *Reveille*, November 26, 1903.

"Tom Horn was hanged at Cheyenne, Wyoming, last Friday. He was condemned to death on a charge of killing a boy named Willie Nickell. It was pretty generally thought that the deed was prompted by cattlemen in whose employ he was at the time the deed was committed, and that he would make a confession implicating others before his death, but he didn't. He went to his death bravely without confession. Newspaper reports a day or two before his death say he confessed killing the boy and expressed sorrow for the act. Up to a day or two of his death, he cherished the hope that his cowboy friends would rescue him before the execution. It is said that "hope springs eternal in the human breast," but it availed nothing in this. Two companies of state militia, with a gatling gun stood guard over the man to prevent any rescue, so he had to die on the scaffold. A biographical sketch of his life says he was born in this county forty-three years ago and that he was a scout with the detachment of regulars that captured Geronimo, the noted Indian Chief, that he served as a government scout for years on the plains under Gen. Miles and was with Miles command in Porto Rico when the Spanish-American war closed."

BIBLIOGRAPHY

"A List of Deaths in Hannibal, MO., 1880-1910: from City of Hannibal & Marion County Records." rev. ed. 1990. Compiled by Roberta & J. Hurley Hagood.

Ballou, Aurelia Pierce and W.F. Cooper. *The Dobyns-Cooper & Allied Families*. Lansing, MI, State Printers, 1908.

Brown, Mabel. "Lawman Joe LeFors Sends Tom Horn to Gallows," *Quarterly of the National Association and Center for Outlaw and Lawmen History*. Vol. VIII, Number 3, Winter, 198-384. pp. 69.

Boulder (CO) *Daily Camera*. November 23, 1903.

Carlson, Chip. *Tom Horn: "Killing men is my specialty...".* Cheyenne, WY, Beartooth Corral, 1991.

_____. "Tom Horn, the Langhoffs, and the 'System That Never Fails'." *True West*. Vol. 40, No. 4., April 1993. pp. 16-21.

Cheyenne Daily Leader. July 24, 1890.

Cheyenne Daily Leader. October 25, 1902.

Davison, Ellen K. *Scotland County, Missouri, U.S.A.: Community At Large, 1993.*

DeMattos, Jack. "Tom Horn," *Real West*. December 1980. pp. 14-17, 49.

Denver Times, Friday Evening, November 20, 1903.

Donoho, Ron. "He Hanged Tom Horn," *The West*. July 1974. pp. 18-20, 55.

"Former Memphis Man Hanged 50 Years Ago," *Memphis (MO) Reveille*. February 19, 1953.

Hagood, J. Hurley, and Roberta Hagood. "Jonathan Pierce: A Family Saga," *Hannibal Courier-Post*. July 2 and July 9, 1994.

Hagood, Mrs. Roberta. "A Letter: Hagood to Larry D. Underwood." November 6, 1995.

_____. "A Letter: Hagood to Larry D. Underwood." November 25, 1995.

Hannibal (Missouri) City Directory: 1873-1916.

Horan, James D. *The Authentic Wild West: The Gunfighters*. NY, Crown Publishers, Inc., 1976.

_____. *The Pinkertons: The Detective Dynasty That Made History*. NY, Bonanza Books, 1967.

"Horn, Tom," *Dictionary of American Biography*. Vol. IX, p. 230. NY, Chas. Scribner's Sons, 1932.

Horn, Tom. *Life of Tom Horn: Written By Himself*. Denver, The Louthan Book Company, 1904.

_____. *Life of Tom Horn: Written By Himself*. Norman, University of Oklahoma Press, 1964.

Krakell, Dean. "Was Tom Horn Two Men?" *True West,. Vol. 17, No. 3., January-February 1970, pp. 12-17, 52-56*.

_____. *The Saga of Tom Horn*. Lincoln, University of Nebraska Press, 1988.

Laramie Bommerang, September 1, 1901.

Launderville, Beulah. "Yours Truly, Tom Horn," *Wyoming State Tribune*. July 22, 1969.

Marion Co. Missouri (Hannibal); Riverside Cemetery. Researched by Tri-County Research, PO Box 1152; Hannibal, n.d.

Memphis (MO) Reveille. November 5, 1903; November 26, 1903; February 19, 1953.

Missouri Obituaries July 1872-73, December 1874. Abstracts of Obituaries Published Weekly in the *St. Louis Christian Advocate*. Compiled by Mrs. Howard E. Woodruff, 1985.

Monaghan, Jay. *The Last of the Bad Men: The Legend of Tom Horn*. Indianapolis, The Bobbs-Merrill Company, 1946.

Paine, Lauran. *Tom Horn: Man of the West*. Barre, MA, Barre Publishing Company, 1963.

"The Real Tom Horn Lies Buried in Boulder Cemetery," *Boulder (CO) Camera*. n.d.

"Reminisce With Leora Peters," *Platte County (WY) Record-Times*. March 13, 1964.

Scotland County Genealogical Society. *Scotland County, Missouri: 1841 Sesquicentennial 1991. Our First 150 Years: Pride in Our Past Confidence in the Future.* 1991.

"Scotland County: Hero or Outlaw?" *Scotland County* (MO) *Democrat.* January 25, 1979.

State-Wide Missouri Obituaries From *The St. Louis Christian Advocate* (Methodist) *1851-1882.* Compiled by Mrs. Howard W. Woodruff, 1986.

"Sweetheart," *The Cincinnati Enquirer.* Sunday, November 1, 1903.

"This Is Anniversary of Most Famous Execution In History of Wyoming," *Wyoming State Tribune.* November 20, 1933.

"Tom Horn: Legends of the West," *True West.* Vol. 43, No. 9. September 1996, p. 31-34.

US Census Records, 1860. Scotland County, Missouri.

US Census Records, 1870. Harrison Township, Scotland County, Missouri.

US Census Records, 1880. Harrison Township, Scotland County, Missouri.

Index

Other books by Larry Underwood available from Dageforde Publishing:

Dreams of Glory: Women of the Old West	$10.95
Love and Glory: Women of the Old West	$10.95
The Custer Fight & Other Tales of the Old West	$9.95
Guns, Gold & Glory	$9.95
Butternut Guerillas	$14.95

Please send:

#	Title	Price	Total

Shipping & Handling: Up to $10.00 - add $3.50; $10.01 - $20.00 add $4.00; $20.01 - $30.00 add $4.50; $30.01 - $45.00 add $5.50; Over $45.00 add $6.00	Total		
	NE residents add 6.5% sales tax		
	Shipping/Handling		
	TOTAL AMOUNT		

Name _____

Address _____

City _____ State _____ Zip _____

Phone ( ) _____

VISA/MasterCard
Account# _____ Exp. Date: _____

Signature _____

(Please clip or photocopy above section)

Send check or money order to:
Dageforde Pubishing, 941 'O' Street, Suite 706
Lincoln, Nebraska 68508-3625 **Or, order toll free: 1-800-216-8794**
Catalog on World Wide Web at www.dageforde.com

Quantity Purchases

Organizations, associations, corporations, hospitals and other groups may qualify for special discounts when ordering more than 24 copies of any title. Please specify quantity desired. Write or call Special Sales Department at Dageforde Publishing.